Also by Arthur Marwick

THE EXPLOSION OF BRITISH SOCIETY 1914–1962
CLIFFORD ALLEN: The Open Conspirator
*THE DELUGE: British Society and the First World War
BRITAIN IN THE CENTURY OF TOTAL WAR: War, Peace and Social Change,
   1900–1967
*THE NATURE OF HISTORY
*THE EXPLOSION OF BRITISH SOCIETY 1914–1970
*WAR AND SOCIAL CHANGE IN THE TWENTIETH CENTURY
THE HOME FRONT: The British and the Second World War
WOMEN AT WAR 1914–1918
CLASS: Image and Reality in Britain, France and the USA since 1930
THE ILLUSTRATED DICTIONARY OF BRITISH HISTORY (*editor*)
BRITISH SOCIETY SINCE 1945
BRITAIN IN OUR CENTURY: Images and Controversies
CLASS IN THE TWENTIETH CENTURY (*editor*)
BEAUTY IN HISTORY: Society, Politics and Personal Appearance, *c*. 1500 to the
   Present

*Also published by Macmillan

Total War and Social Change

Edited by
Arthur Marwick

MACMILLAN
PRESS

First published 1988 by
THE MACMILLAN PRESS LTD
Houndmills, Basingstoke, Hampshire RG21 2XS
and London
Companies and representatives
throughout the world

ISBN 0–333–45590–8 hardcover
ISBN 0–333–45591–6 paperback

A catalogue record for this book is available
from the British Library.

Printed in Hong Kong

Reprinted 1994

Contents

List of Tables

Notes on the Contributors

François Bédarida, after graduating at the University of Paris (Ecole Normale Supérieure, Agrégation d'Histoire), taught modern history successively at the French Institute in London, and at the Sorbonne and the Institute d'Etudes Politiques in Paris. He was Director of the Maison Française d'Oxford from 1966 to 1971. Since 1979 he has been Director of Research at the Centre National de la Recherche Scientifique and Director of the Institut d'Histoire du Temps Présent. His recent publications include *A social history of England, 1850–1975; La stratégie secrète de la drôle de guerre; La bataille d'Angleterre; Will Thorne: la voie anglaise du socialisme; Normandie 1944: du débarquement à la libération.*

Paul Dukes is Reader in History at the University of Aberdeen where he has been since 1964. He is the author of several works on Russian, comparative Russian–American and European History.

James F. McMillan teaches History at the University of York. He prepared a D Phil thesis at the University of Oxford under the supervision of Richard Cobb on 'The Effects of the First World War on the Social Condition of Women in France' (1976), Among his publications are two books, *Housewife or Harlot: the Place of Women in French Society 1870–1940* and *Dreyfus to De Gaulle: Politics and Society in France 1898–1969.*

Wolfgang J. Mommsen is Professor of Modern History at the University of Düsseldorf and has held posts at Cornell University, Ithaca, N. Y., the Institute for Advanced Study, Princeton, the Free University in Amsterdam, the School of Advanced International Studies of John Hopkins University, Washington, DC. From 1977 to 1985 he was Director of the German Historical Institute London, and also from 1981 to 1985 visiting Professor at the London School of Economics. He is Secretary-General of the International Commission of History of Historiography and treasurer of the Verband der Historiker Deutschlands. In 1987 he was awarded a D Litt by the University of East Anglia.

He has published widely on Max Weber, and his book *Max Weber und die deutsche Politik* is available in English. He has also published numerous books and articles on problems of European Imperialism, on German and British history in the nineteenth and twentieth centuries, and on problems of history of historiography and theory of history.

Alastair Reid is Fellow, Tutor and Director of Studies in History at Girton College, Cambridge. He is the author of a number of important articles on British social and labour history, and is currently working on a study of trade unions in the shipbuilding industry between 1870 and 1940.

Mark Roseman is a lecturer in the Modern Languages department at Aston University. He has just completed a doctorate at the University of Warwick on 'New Miners in the Ruhr' and has written a number of articles and papers on the history of the Ruhr and on Germany's reconstruction after 1945.

Penny Summerfield lectures in the social history of education at the University of Lancaster. She is author of *Women Workers in the Second World War* and co-author (with Gail Braybon) of *Out of the Cage: Women's Experiences in Two World Wars*. Since 1981 she has also published articles on various aspects of the Second World War, such as education and politics in the armed forces, women and welfare, the 'levelling of class' and the activities of Mass Observation. She is currently working on a project on the oral history of childhood and schooling in the period 1900–50.

Preface

The individual chapters of this book were first presented to a conference on Total War and Social Change held at the Open University in January 1987. I wish to record my deepest thanks to the British Academy for the grant which made possible the participation of the two distinguished continental scholars, François Bédarida and Wolfgang Mommsen. I would also like to thank the Vice-Chancellor, Dr J. H. Horlock, and the Deputy Vice-Chancellor, Professor Norman Gowar, for making available the basic funds necessary for this conference, John Martin, General Facilities Manager at the Open University, Wendy Simpson, who carried out the detailed organisation for the conference, Gill Wood, who assisted with registration and allied matters, and also typed the Introduction and Conclusion, my translation of Professor Bédarida's chapter, and prepared the entire typescript for the press, and my colleagues Clive Emsley and Tony Lentin who shared the (agreeable) duties of chairing the conference sessions. Most of all, of course, I must thank the distinguished contributors to this volume; but also, indeed, all of those who participated in what was widely recognised as a most successful and highly coherent conference, including the four other speakers, Professor Norman Stone of Oxford, Dr Paul Addison of Edinburgh, and Drs David Englander and Anthony Aldgate of the Open University, all of whom presented stimulating and informative addresses.

ARTHUR MARWICK

Introduction
Arthur Marwick

Wars loom large in the memories of ordinary human beings; particularly this is true of those who have directly encountered the intense excitement, as well as the dreadful tragedy and suffering, of war, who have been projected by war into new jobs, new experiences, and, perhaps, a new sense of purpose and self-esteem, or who have been swayed by the claims both of government propagandists and idealistic activists that the horror and sacrifice of war must necessarily lead to the creation of a better world. Even if those personally involved in the second of the twentieth century's total wars are now passing from the scene, younger generations still absorb national myths, mainly through television and simplified text books; and they still feel the perennial fascination exerted by tales of human slaughter on a massive scale. Thus they continue (if they have any views on the matter at all) to perceive the two world wars as major 'land marks' or 'turning points' (the subject readily lends itself to cliché) in the development of twentieth-century society. It is the pleasure and passion of professional historians to explode myths and chastise the common reader for his or her simple beliefs.

Certainly, most of the academic writing of the last decade or so has dedicated itself to the propositions that such social change as has taken place in the twentieth century has been a product of long-term processes and not of war, that the wars, if anything, have obstructed rather than fostered change, and that those contemporaries who enthused over the changes they believed war to be bringing about were, lacking the hindsight and the wisdom of the historian, simply mistaken. Surprisingly, especially since it is widely understood in educational circles that there is a 'controversy' or 'debate' over whether the two wars did have identifiable social consequences, this writing is not very extensive, most of it concentrating not only on single countries, but on single issues within these countries (the status of women is, of course, a favourite). There are a few international studies (principally by Ferro, Hardach, Wright, Schmitt and myself[1]); Britain has been quite thoroughly scrutinised (myself, Winter, Wilson, Waites, Calder, Addison, and the collection edited by Smith); only in late 1986 did Wynn's study of the United States and World War I join the earlier treatment of World War II by Polenberg (I speak here solely of serious scholarly studies, and studies dealing with social change as distinct from political and military events); Kocka's World War I study, *Facing Total War*, in fact very largely confines itself to the lower middle class, and while Feldman's *Army, Industry and Labor* is suggestive and wide-ranging it does not claim to be a comprehensive study; the later period, as Mark Roseman points out, has been dominated by studies of Nazism to the exclusion of comprehensive studies of the war itself as social experience; there are no *complete* studies of Austria–Hungary and World War I, and the situation is similar for France and Italy in respect of both wars, though, of course much invaluable work has been done on women and labour in World War I and on the Resistance in World War II;[2] studies of the Russian Revolutions are legion, but of the war itself as a social phenomenon practically non-existent; nor is there much, as Paul Dukes indicates, on World War II. Crucial contributions to the wider debates have been made by Milward, though his orientation has been largely, though not exclusively, economic.[3]

Personal memory, the rhetoric of politicians and reformers, national myths: all of these are poor guides to whether wars do have significant social consequences. Yet clearly the issue does merit systematic investigation. If individuals themselves feel that their attitudes and aspirations have been transformed by their war experiences, and if politicians do initiate new social legislation, then these in themselves are social consequences, if only minor ones. Much more than that: World War I was accompanied, in Russia, by radical revolution, and, in Germany and Austria–Hungary, by revolutions of more limited character. Throughout Europe new social reforms were enacted and new rights for labour enshrined (most notably in the Treaty of Versailles itself); most countries – though not France – granted political rights to women. The transformations, on the surface at least, were as great at the end of World War II: democracy restored to Germany, 'welfare state' legislation widely introduced, rapidly rising living standards replacing the depressed conditions of the inter-war years, women at last getting the vote in France. Now, as is repeatedly, and very reasonably, pointed out, just because changes *accompanied* or *followed* war, that does not automatically mean that they were *caused* by war. But we do have a *prima facie* case for an investigation; one might very properly wish to find out why so many changes came during or immediately after war, and not earlier or later, and why they came, as it were, in a bunch, and not spread out as tends to be more normal, certainly in the case of major social and political legislation.

When I first set out upon my own investigations in the early 1960s (I fear that the nature of this enterprise, and my own long-term involvement in it, pushes me towards being less self-effacing than is proper in an editor), I was, in addition, strongly motivated by the fact that at that time almost all studies of war concentrated solely on the military and political aspects: my *The Deluge: British Society and the First World War* (1965) sought to redress the balance by giving due weight to the domestic and social side (there is, as I have just indicated, much work, across many countries, still to be done here). My efforts quickly developed in two directions. First, since it did seem to me clear that certain social changes definitely were related to the experience of war, I became preoccupied with the question of showing as systematically as possible *why* this should be so; I found myself increasingly dissatisfied with argument by metaphor, as in the assertion that 'war *accelerates* existing trends' – if this is so (and I very much doubt that it is in *every* instance) the real question, I felt, was, once more, *why* wars should have this alleged accelerating effect.[4] Second, I soon moved into the field of comparative study: I felt that if one looked at how different countries reacted to, and were affected by, the same wars, one would both learn a great deal about the nature of war, and illuminate vital differences in the nature of the different societies themselves; for such an ambitious study one needs a basic framework, and this was provided by the theory I had developed on the question of how involvement in war *may* (not necessarily *will*) produce social change. Probably *War and Social Change in the Twentieth Century* (1974), useful pioneering work though I still believe it to have been, was too ambitious in attempting comparative coverage of Britain, France, Germany, Russia, and the United States in the space of 250 pages, with the result that certain of my pronouncements were overly condensed and insufficiently nuanced. In the dozen or so years since (while also devoting myself to other major areas of research) I have continued to develop and refine my arguments.[5] Penny Summerfield, in the final chapter of this book, remarks that I have 'modified' my 'earlier position': I would myself rather say that I have *clarified* it, responding, as any historian who does not confuse scholarship with the unyielding defence of a prepared position, must do, to new evidence and to the arguments of colleagues.

Two points I must insist on: never, in any of my writings have I sought to deny – what an appalling historian I would be if I did – the importance of long-term processes of change, both structural and ideological, nor have I at any time confined my studies to war-time and the immediate post war years, thus failing, as has been alleged, to sort out which changes, if any, were truly lasting from the purely temporary ones. Consistently in all of my studies I start with a full analysis of society as it was on the eve of war and finish with one of how society was once it had settled down *after* the immediate post-war period, making it clear the 'the comparison one has to make is not simply between post-war and pre-war society, but between post-war society and the situation that society would have reached at the same point in time had there been no war.'[6] War, I have quite explicitly stated in my earliest writings, 'is not the only, nor is it the most important instrument of change', adding that 'in all twentieth-century industrialised societies the pressures generated by the unguided activities of individuals and groups within these societies, mightily assisted by the resources of science and technology, have been towards a greater share for the many of economic and material well-being, social status and political responsibility', with change being further fostered by deliberate political action based on paternalist, liberal, socialist, or other ideological principles.[7] In the opening chapter of *War and Social Change* it was stated quite unambiguously that 'there would be no point in studying the effects of war on any society without first grasping firmly the essential features of that society, the processes of change already in motion within that society on the eve of war'.[8]

Having made these points, I feel bound to add that I consider that the historian who puts everything down to long-term trends, who maintains that everything that happened would have happened anyway, is abdicating his or her responsibility to explain why a particular development took place *when* it did, and in the *way* it did. The ultimate concern of the historian is not with what might have happened, or what would have happened, but with what actually did happen. The purely temporary and short-term must, of course, be winnowed out from the lasting and long-term, and, of course, the latter is much more worthy of attention than the former. But it is important, too, to remember that historians are concerned with the lives of real human beings. Within the short life-spans allotted to us all, it may matter very much indeed whether child welfare clinics are introduced when we are 22 or 37, or the right to study for the bar when we are leaving school or when we are about to retire, or decent living standards at one point in time or twenty years later. To me there is something inhuman about historians who rattle on for ever about long-term trends without ever looking at immediate human consequences. There can be no doubt about the clustering around the two world wars of quite notable social changes: the question does require answering as to whether, and how, the timing was affected by war. Change, incidentally, is neutral: it can have adverse as well as beneficial effects on individuals and groups of human beings. This issue, too, is not well understood, there being historians who equate change with what they understand as 'progressive change'.[9] Later in this book Paul Dukes remarks succinctly with regard to Russia and World War II, 'total war, both hot and cold, had led to a more complete totalitarianism.' Regrettable, but change all the same.

There has never been any ambiguity as to what I mean by social change: first, changes in *social geography*, including population, urbanisation and distribution of industry; second, *economic and technological* change, including changes in theory and structures; third, changes in *social structure*; fourth changes in *social cohesion*, particularly with regard to national and racial minorities; fifth, changes in *social welfare and social policy*; sixth, changes in *material conditions*; seventh, changes in *customs and behaviour*; eighth, changes in *artistic and intellectual ideas and practices and in popular culture*; ninth, changes *in the family and in the role and status of women*; tenth, changes in *social and political values, institutions and ideas*.[10] Why might total war bring change in all or some of these areas? In my view it is not helpful to think of war as some discrete entity 'out there' which, at certain periods, 'impacts' on society. War, alas, *is* a human and social activity, as much as digging coal or making windy political speeches. We have to envisage a continuum, 'society at war'. We are then at once in a position to compare 'society at war' with 'society not at war'. If we do this carefully and conscientiously, we begin to notice that in 'society at war' certain activities take place, certain situations are created, certain problems arise, certain processes are set in motion, not present in 'society not at war'. These activities, processes, etc., interact to touch off all kinds of mechanisms of change, direct and indirect, few completely new, most in the form of intensification (hence the effect of 'acceleration') or distortion of ideas and developments already present. Aspects of society are transformed; there is no certainty that these transformations will last beyond the immediate war period save that one of the processes apparent in 'society at war' predisposes society towards preserving some of the war-time innovations and against returning absolutely to things as they were before. There is created a *potential* for long-term change, though how matters actually work out will depend on a large number of other factors.

In my endeavour to pin down the exact nature of the processes brought in to play in a 'society at war', I have suggested breaking the complex inter-relationship between society and its experience of the war it is itself waging into four headings or 'dimensions'. These, inevitably, overlap; the exact number, and the exact phrasing is not important: others might well find better ways of expressing the basic idea – and it is the basic idea, that of what happens in 'society at war' that does not happen in 'society not at war' – which is crucial in explaining *why* wars *may* bring about change. The four dimensions, I should stress, do not form a framework for this book: from time to time authors do refer, quite probably without conscious allusion to my own writings, to one or other of them, but basically they adopt their own approaches to the question they were asked to address: 'In what ways, if any, has Total War been critical in bringing about significant Social Change?' Nonetheless it will, I believe, help to illuminate the general issue, to which the chapters which follow are specific contributions, and to establish the basic content of *War and Social Change*, to which there *are* several references in this book, if (continuing to eschew editorial self-effacement) I briefly set out the four 'dimensions'.

First, the *destructive* and *disruptive* dimension of war. Clearly in its direct implications this entails regression rather than change in any acceptable sense of the term. However, destruction in itself creates an impulse towards re-building, and, as social science studies of natural disaster have suggested, sometimes this can mean an impulse towards re-building better than before. Disruption can result in old patterns of behaviour (as, say, in remote rural villages) being replaced by new ones (young men deciding to settle in the cities, say); it can result in projecting people into new situations or in offering them opportunities they would not have had in peacetime (as with war work for women).

Second is the *test* dimension. No value judgements are involved here, for it is certainly not being argued that 'higher' forms of social organisation, whatever that may mean, 'pass' the test, while 'lower' ones fail. The argument merely is that, manifestly, wars impose enormous stresses and strains to which a country's military, social, political and economic institutions must adapt if the country is to avoid defeat; indeed if the institutions are grossly inadequate they will collapse, as in Tsarist Russia. For most countries involved in total war the experience has tested, among other things, the cruder fallacies of economic liberalism, the procedures for exploiting the full potential of science and technology, the bonds between State and people, and the welfare provisions for the weaker members of the community. In many cases the *test*, in its various forms, may have highly undesirable outcomes: apart from collapse (which could itself have disagreeable effects) the stresses and challenges of waging war might well produce dictatorship, secret police, censorship, or, at least, centralisation and secrecy, as well as, or instead of, social reform. The concern, to repeat, is with change, not simply with 'progressive' change.

Third is the *participation* dimension. Total war requires the involvement, whether in the army or on the domestic front, of hitherto underprivileged groups (such as the working class, women, ethnic minorities). Such participation will provide the *possibility* of social gains, or, at a minimum, of developing new consciousness and self-esteem. At bottom this is because those who are *in* demand are in a strong market position to press *their* demands; it may also be the case that governments will seek to reward essential workers, or maintain their morale by offering social reform. Alastair Reid, in Chapter 2, makes fruitful use of this argument, though (unwisely in my view) he retains Andreski's original formulation, *Military Participation Ratio*.[11] However Reid does most usefully elaborate the basic concept by breaking it down into three sub-sets: economic (bargaining in the changed market place), institutional (unions bargaining with employers), and consultation with the State. He is also, surely, absolutely right to stress that the participation effect is not automatic. However in my view the very nature and condition of participation must also be closely scrutinised:[12] those who respond freely to market opportunities on the home front are much more likely to be in a position to make gains than those who are conscripted into the war front.

Fourth is the *psychological* dimension. War is an enormous emotional experience, during which loyalty towards one's own group, or those with whom one comes to identify in wartime (one's trade union, the working class, other women, the entire nation) intensifies, as does hostility to 'out-groups' (principally, of course, the enemy). Considerable force is also given to the notion (there is plenty of evidence of this) that such appalling slaughter must be *for* something, that change in many spheres, including the cultural, must eventuate. The special horrors of war, in any case, call forth new intellectual and artistic responses.[13]

On the basis that war calls forth such responses, I have argued that, within the wider context set by secular structural and ideological trends, certain long-term developments, in the precise manner and timing in which they came about, can be directly attributed to the experience of war. I see these changes as being, to a large degree, 'unguided', rather than brought about by the conscious volition of politicians; as Paul Addison has put it, with reference to Britain and World War II: 'Then as now, it was a fiction that governments make society. Society makes governments, and unmakes them too.'[14] As already stressed, it is vitally important to be clear about the nature of the society one is studying, as it was on the eve of war. If war has not brought to Britain the cataclysmic changes experienced by, say, Russia or Japan, this is largely because in 1914 Britain was already an advanced industrial society with flexible representative (thought not democratic) institutions. So also it is essential to take into account the different intensities with which a war impinges on the different societies studied:[15] invasion, devastation, occupation, defeat, at one extreme, bombed but inviolate Britain, and untouched America at the other – the different chapters in this book bring out the contrasts most effectively.

These views, as noted above, are not in the high tide of fashion at the moment. In Chapter 7, Penny Summerfield refers to those who now dominate the literature as 'the revisionists'. Actually historical debate does not proceed in orderly succession of proposition, revision, etc. Angus Calder and Henry Pelling were very early presenting the case that war did not have positive social consequences,[16] while two very recent books have strongly argued to the contrary.[17] My own personal view is that out of their own mouths the 'revisionists', being the excellent historians that they are, actually show that the wars *did* have certain clearly identifiable consequences, despite their own vehement insistence that their evidence proves the exact opposite.[18] It is further my personal view that the 'revisionists' take this line primarily for ideological reasons. Most of them are feminists, or socialists, or both, and therefore believe in the possibility of the total transformation of society, resulting in the abolition of all inequalities of sex and class. Judged by such standards, the consequences of the two wars indeed seem puny; judged (as I would judge them) by the context of the times, they are perhaps less negligible (an interesting consideration, well brought out by James McMillan, is that feminists today put a much more profound meaning to the term 'emancipation' than was the case in the earlier part of the century). It is, further, a canon of faith to the 'revisionists' that change can only come from the conscious action of militants, taking control themselves, or forcing concessions from the` ruling class: thus they discount the unguided changes of which I have spoken. The 'revisionists' also, in a broadly Marxist way, attribute overriding importance to long-term structural change, or to revolution: the contingencies of war do not fit easily into this programme. Finally, in taking single topics, they miss the complex interactions inherent in society's involvement in the war it is waging. (Women got the vote in Britain in 1918 in the first instance because many men also had to be enfranchised;[19] in France *all* men already had the vote, so that factor did not operate).

However, the contributions of the 'revisionists', working usually from previously unavailable documents, and frequently bringing a fresh feminist perspective into play, have been immense. The debate now focuses very much upon the precise balance to be struck, in different contexts, between long-term and short-term factors and outcomes, and between those who maintain that *some* significant changes are discernible, and those who insist that war's effects are overwhelmingly negative and regressive, Martin Pugh being a leading proponent of this view with respect to women's franchise and World War I Britain.[20] Interestingly, the latest challenge to Pugh has come from a feminist writer, Sandra Holton.[21]

This book follows no particular line. Perhaps I have exceeded my rights as editor in expatiating on my own views. But then I have always maintained that historical writing should be 'a dialogue between the historian and his audience'.[22] The historian should state his or her assumptions, and display the evidence: readers may then form their own conclusions. As a matter of fact the first and last chapters of this book are written by two of my most vigorous and persuasive critics, James McMillan and Penny Summerfield (good friends and respected colleagues both; I have never understood why intellectual disagreement should spill over into personal animosity). Several of the other authors do not refer at all to my arguments. The essential strength of each chapter, in fact, is that it establishes, in the light of the latest research and, in particular, through the assiduous use of statistics, exactly what did happen in the country studied, resolving vexed problems relating to levels of economic activity, employment of women, and the exact numbers executed in the *épuration* (the purging of collaborators at the end of World War II in France). Though the British scene is the one most worked over, both Alastair Reid and Penny Summerfield add important evidence and perceptive insights. The chapters by Wolfgang Mommsen and Mark Roseman (Germany), Paul Dukes (Russia) and François Bédarida (France) all relate directly to the great ideological movements of twentieth-century Europe: for instance, Mommsen, among many other matters (including Kocka's thesis about World War I and class) discusses the origins of Nazism, while Roseman discusses its legacy. Both Roseman and Dukes stress the importance of international influences on social change, the latter writing that: 'Some superficial appearances and, indeed, some deeper realities notwithstanding, the external relationships with the United States and the rest of the world quickly became a governing influence on the manner in which the road to Communism was resumed.' The Soviet Union, of course, provides the prime example of war as cataclysm. The contrasts and comparisons with the two British chapters are highly instructive in connection with the case (mine) that total war is one single phenomenon, though in many types.

Each chapter provides a slightly different answer to the basic question. This is mainly because of the unique characteristics of the individual country studied and the particular way in which total war impinged on it; it is partly also because of the particular assumptions of the individual author. I shall not follow the boring practice of giving a potted summary of each contribution. I have said too much; so now let each distinguished authority speak for himself and herself. In a brief Conclusion I shall seek to highlight some of the more striking points relating directly to the themes set out in this Introduction.

Notes

1. For the books referred to here and in the remainder of this sentence see the general annotated bibliography at the end of the book.
2. See in particular Patrick Fridenson (ed.) *1914–1918: l'Autre Front* (Paris, 1977); and the many works on the French Resistance by Henri Michel.
3. Alan Milward, *The German Economy at War* (1965), *The New Order and the French Economy* (1970), *The Economic Effects of the Two World Wars on Britain* (1970), *War, Economy and Society, 1939–1945* (1977).
4. My first shot was published as 'The Impact of the First World War on British Society', in the *Journal of Contemporary History*, III (January, 1968), which was shortly followed by *Britain in the Century of Total War; War, Peace and Social Change 1900–1967* (1968).
5. Principally in 'People's War and Top People's Peace? British Society and the Second World War', in Alan Sked and Chris Cook (eds) *Crisis*

and Controversy: Essays in Honour of A. J. P. Taylor (1976), pp. 148–64, and papers delivered to the Anglo-Dutch Conference on War and Society (1976), published as 'World War II and Social Class in Britain' in A. C. Duke and C. A. Tamse (eds) *Britain and the Netherlands*, vol. VI (1977) pp. 203–27; to the Royal Military College, Canada, (1980) published as 'Problems and Consequences of Organizing Society for Total War' in N. F. Dreisziger (ed.) *Mobilization for Total War: The Canadian, American and British Experience 1914–1918*, pp. 3–21; to the American Air Force College (1982), published as 'Total War and Social Change in Britain and the other European Countries', USAF Academy, *Tenth Military History Symposium: The Home Front and War in the Twentieth Century* (Colorado, 1984); and to the Social History Society, published (in brief summary) as 'Total War and Social Change: Myths and Misunderstandings' in *Social History Society Newsletter* (1984). See also *Class: Image and Reality in Britain, France and the USA since 1930* (London, 1980), chs 11 and 12 and *Britain in Our Century: Images and Controversies* (1984) chs 2 and 5.

6. Arthur Marwick *War and Social Change in the Twentieth Century: a comparative study of Britain, France, Germany, Russian and the United States* p. 222.

7. Arthur Marwick *Britain in the Century of Total War: War, Peace and Social Change, 1900–1967*, p. 16.

8. *War and Social Change in the Twentieth Century*, p. 14.

9. See John Macnicol, 'The effect of the evacuation of schoolchildren on official attitudes to State intervention', in H. L. Smith (ed.) *War and Social Change: British Society in the Second World War* (1986) p. 3.

10. *War and Social Change in the Twentieth Century*, p. 13; *British Society Since 1945* (1982) pp. 19–20

11. Stanislaw Andreski, *Military Organisation and Society* (1954), pp. 33-8.

12. *War and Social Change in the Twentieth Century*, pp. 219,223; Ian Beckett, in Ian F. W. Beckett and Keith Simpson (eds), *A Nation in Arms: A social study of the British army in the First World War* (Manchester, 1985) p. 27, has perceptively suggested that 'conceivably, wars change societies more than the armies that defend them.' See also David Englander, 'The French Soldier 1914–18', *French History*, vol 1, no. 1 (1987) pp. 49–67.

13. For some brief thoughts, see *War and Social Change*, pp. 83–6. The classic study of war's effects on the literary consciousness is Paul Fussel, *The Great War in Modern Memory* (1975).

14. Paul Addison, *Now the War is Over* (1985) p. vii.

15. *War and Social Change in the Twentieth Century*, p. 14.

16. Angus Calder, *The People's War* (1969); Henry Pelling, *Britain in the Second World War* (1970).

17. Jay Winter, *The Great War and the British People* (1985); Neil A. Wynn, *From progressivism to Prosperity: America and World War I* (New York, 1986).

18. See my Social History Society paper, and also my review in the *Times Higher Educational Supplement*, 6 March, 1987. For main 'revisionist' works see annotated general bibliography.

19. For a summary see my *Women at War 1914–1918* (1977) pp. 152–7; see also Martin Pugh, *Electoral Reform in War and Peace, 1906–1918*(1978) ch 10.
20. Pugh, *Electoral Reform*, and *Women's Suffrage in Britain, 1867–1928* (1980).
21. Sandra Stanley Holton, *Feminism and Democracy: Women's Suffrage and Reform Politics in Britain, 1900–1918* (1986), pp. 147–8; also p. 116.
22. *Britain in the Century of Total War*, p. 11.

1 World War I and Women in France

James F. McMillan

ʃrectcheri e

In analysing social change, French historians tend to attach more importance to trends and developments which take place over the long term (the *longue durée*) than to individual 'events'. British historians, while not insensitive to such secular trends, more readily concede that 'events' – especially when they are as cataclysmic as World War I – may play a determining role in their own right. It is the particular achievement of Professor Arthur Marwick to have made the relationship between total war and social change one of the key problems of contemporary historiography. My own position will be seen to be closer to that of the French historians: but I should say at the outset that I in no way dispute Professor Marwick's central proposition, namely that World War I is a privileged vantage point from which to observe social change.[1] The war gives us a precise moment on which to focus, an opportunity, as it were, to take stock and assess the relative importance of war-time innovations when set beside long-term change and continuities.

Our differences arise once we set about the actual business of evaluating the processes of change. Professor Marwick's method is to concentrate on the war years themselves, on the not unreasonable assumption that a society at war differs from a society not at war and that the historian's task is to examine precisely how these differ: in this way he is free to emphasise all the novelties introduced by the war-time situation. The procedure is fine as far as it goes: without knowing what happened during the war we are in no position to assess its overall impact. The trouble with the Marwick approach is that it does not go far enough. By definition, war is an *exceptional* state and in addition to what happened during the war we need to know what happened afterwards. In other words, how many of the war-time changes survived into peace-time and the return to 'normality'? Did war bring about *lasting* social change?

To establish this, it is necessary to show that the war decisively altered a pre-existing situation and produced a new post-war norm. Such a demonstration is only possible by examining the problem from

1

a perspective that includes not just the war years but the years both before and after 1914. In the latter case one would want to distinguish further the *immediate* post-war years (1919–20), when the picture is somewhat confused with demobilisation and the removal of war-time controls and, say, the mid-1920s, when post-war patterns have become reasonably clear and settled. Only then can meaningful comparisons with the pre-war period be drawn and the nature and extent of change over the long term measured. The perspective of the *longue durée* also safeguards against the facile but false *post hoc, propter hoc* árgument – that change which took place after the war necesarily took place on account of the war.

What, in any case, is signified by the term 'social change'? Surely, to be helpful, it has to amount to something more than temporary dislocations to normal existence resulting from the exigencies of war. Rather, it suggest perceptible and durable transformations in social structures, social relations and social organisation. To claim that World War I was responsible for decisive social change in France is to assert that, as a result of war, French society in the inter-war years was qualitatively and recognisably different from what it had been in the so-called *Belle Epoque*. For the French, World War I was a tragic and traumatic experience, leaving deep psychological scars: they were a sadder people in the 1920s than they had been in the 1900s. Few historians, however, believe that the social structures of the Third Repulic were radically transformed over the first three decades of the twentieth century. Total war did not produce total change. In so far as change did take place, not all of it could be attributed to the war. What we need, therefore, is a nuanced analysis which will do justice to the respects in which France *was* different and which will weigh up carefully the part played by war in contributing to change. *Prima facie*, it would seem prudent to assume that change did not proceed evenly and that some people were more affected by the war than others – a *caveat* that applies as much to women as to men.

On the subject of women, a final word of clarification is in order before trying to work out how they were affected by World War I. It is frequently alleged that the war 'emancipated' women.[2] The notion of 'emancipation', however, is fraught with ambiguity. Its connotations in 1914 were not those which would be understood today by radical feminists. At the time it was generally taken to imply 'equal rights' for women: that is, civic equality, the same political rights as men and access to educational and employment opportunities on the same terms as men – in a word, to equality in the public sphere.[3] Today, 'emancipation' carries wider implications of sexual freedom: it denotes 'autonomy', the right of women to determine their own destinies, free from any gender-based constraints. The contemporary and more restricted usage is the easier to measure: present-day criteria may not be entirely applicable to the period in question and may well unjustifiably belittle such change as did take place. After all, by the standards acceptable to late-twentieth-century radical feminists, women's 'emancipation' is still a long way off. Here it will be assumed that any notable change – in the law, in political rights, in employment opportunities or in attitudes – constitutes a shift in the direction of autonomy and contributed if not to the complete 'emancipation' of women, then to an amelioration of their social condition.

World War I inevitably impinged on the lives of French women since they constituted more than 50 per cent of the French population and France as a nation was profoundly affected by the war. Over 1.3 million men died. Another 3 million were wounded. The northern and eastern soil of France witnessed some of the bloodiest battles of the war, with disastrous consequences for industry and agriculture as well as humen life. Prices rose by at least 400 per cent. The public debt quintupled. For the French nation, the war was a material and moral calamity. The illusions of victory may have provided some (short-lived) consolation, but the French people could not escape from the knowledge that a terrible catastrophe had befallen them. In that respect, post-war France was a very different place from the France of the *fin-de siécle*.

Most French men and women at the time of World War I were peasants, and rural France bore the brunt of the human disaster. 700 000 peasant soldiers perished (42 per cent of the total dead): another 500 000 were wounded. Yet, in spite of the frightening carnage, it could be argued that, for the survivors, in some ways the situation of the countryside was improved by the war. Inflation, so harmful to the *rentier* and all who worked for a fixed wage or salary, was a boon to peasant proprietors, releasing them from chronic indebtedness and introducing them to relative prosperity, all the more so as prices for their produce continued to rise in the 1920s. Townspeople were not slow to denounce post-war peasants as a class of *nouveaux riches* and war profiteers.[4]

Peasant women obviously shared in the general upturn in the fortunes of the peasantry as a whole. In that sense, they could be said to have gained from the war. Whether the war did anything to improve the situation of rural women *qua* women is an altogether different matter. Nineteenth-century rural society certainly had an ideology of male dominance, expressed in many sayings and proverbs, for example:

The death of a wife is not a disaster, but the death of a cow is. (Alsace)

A soft pear and a silent woman are both good. (Anjou)[5]

But the idea that the peasant woman had an essentially domestic role, leaving men to work the fields and act as sole producers is a myth, invented largely by urban folklorists. As the excellent study by Martine Segalen shows, women were crucial to the running of a peasant farm and were full partners in the economic enterprise. As well as their maternal and household tasks they performed chores vital to the farm's output, and, when necessary, were expected to take over from men. Thus, when women replaced men in the fields during World War I, they did so 'with an ease which was surprising only to those who had seen them simply as bougeois women transplanted to the fields. They took on the management and upkeep of the farm just as they had done throughout their lives, when their husbands died or emigrated.'[6] When the men came back, the women resumed their customary tasks. In that sense, the lot of peasant women was unchanged by the war. In the longer term, it was to be technological change, above all the mechanisation of agriculture, which transformed relations between the sexes in the countryside, depriving women of their traditionally productive role and channelling them towards a more private and domestic world.

Urban women would appear to be a more promising object of study than peasant women for the social historian investigating the relationship between war and social change in France at the time of World War I.[7] Contemporaries were rightly impressed by the scale of women's contribution to the war effort, above all by the massive mobilisation of a female labour force. By 1916, it had become official government policy to substitute women workers for absent men wherever possible. In chemicals, in transport, but especially in the munitions factories, women came to constitute a crucial element in the work force. In the whole of France, women provided a quarter of the personnel in the war factories, a figure which rose to 362 879 women in a total labour force of 1 580 459 workers. In the Paris region, which accounted for 40 per cent of all French war production, women made up about a third of the work force in metallurgical industries. Overall, the expansion of female labour in metalworking was of the order of 900 per cent. Many of the new women workers either had no previous experience of factory work or came from the traditional 'feminine' sectors of the labour force (the clothing industry, domestic service and textiles). In the tertiary sector, women replaced men as secretaries and clerical workers, teachers and civil servants, even as doctors. At the same time, new opportunities began to open up in nursing, midwifery and social work.

Women's war work came in for constant contemporary comment – most, but not all, of it favourable. The principal recurring theme was that work would have a liberating effect on women, dramatically altering their place in society in the post-war world. On the one hand, they would gain from new employment opportunities: on the other hand, they would benefit from an enhanced self-confidence and from new social attitudes towards women's role. Writing in *Le Revue Hebdomadaire* (22 July 1916), a woman journalist predicted that the war would lead to an 'upheaval in the social order' and a 'shift in values'.[8] The feminist leader Jane Misme agreed. The war, according to her, was bound to bring a number of changes but 'the main change will be that in the feminine attitude towards work'.[9] Another commentator declared that even if women – especially bourgeois women – wanted to return to the pre-1914 situation, this was impossible: their role in the labour force had become too crucial.[10] The Director of the Conservatoire National des Art-et-Métiers expressed the change in this way:

> The point of knowing whether women should be able to accede to posts until now reserved to men no longer needs examining. Feminism has gained its cause . . . The war will have the effect of bringing down all the barriers still maintained for entry to careers where, to this point, men alone have developed their effort of intellectual and material production.

According to Léon Abensour, an early historian of the French feminist movement, women made more progress during World War I than they had done in fifty years of struggle.[12] The academic lawyer and conservative politician Joseph Barthélemy was of like mind, including France in his observation that 'in a great many countries the war has accomplished rapid and extraordinary progress for the cause of sex equality'.[13]

A frequent refinement of the theme was that middle-class women would be more affected by the war than working-class women. The latter, after all, usually had some experience of the world of work, whereas for bourgeois women, accustomed to lives of domesticity, work was a novelty. In future, proclaimed an article in *Le Revue* (May 1917), 'woman will no longer be a creature of luxury. Tomorrow there will be work for everybody. The reign of woman as plaything, ignorant of life and its difficulties, happy with her molly-coddled existence, is over.'[14] In similar vein, another commentator wrote that upper-class women, hitherto interested mainly in their own pleasure, now knew what it was to have to work to live. Consequently they had acquired 'more initiative, more decisiveness, a more practical sense, more varied knowledge'.[15] Another writer, while agreeing that the new emphasis on work would lead to the emancipation of the bourgeois woman, warned that the process of adjustment would be difficult. Like the working-class woman who had sacrificed her husband, the bourgeois woman had lost a loved one: but in her case he was not only '*l'être-aimé*' but everything – '*l'être-aimé et la situation*'. Only a lucky minority would be able to remarry or adapt to the new order of things through the possession of some special talent: the rest faced considerable hardship.[16]

Even opponents of women's work and apologists for the ideal of *la femme au foyer* ('woman by the hearth') were resigned to change. Henri Joly, writing in *Le Correspondant*, observed that women's natural role was in the home and that women's work in factories in the nineteenth century had often been carried out in appalling conditions. Nevertheless, France was short of labour, and women would be required to assist in the work of reconstruction, just as they had been needed for the war effort.[17] F. Lepelletier, an apologist for traditionalist Catholic social doctrines, deplored the fact that women were obliged to work during the war: both 'the future of the race' and moral standards were thereby compromised. Yet even he saw no alternative, at least for the duration of the war. By 1919 he was lamenting that what was supposed to have been a temporary situation looked like becoming permanent: a re-education programme would be necessary to convince women that their foremost obligation to society was as wives and mothers.[18]

Not everyone was so gloomy at the prospect of a new social role for French women. One commentator rejoiced that the war would liberate all women, not just those whose husbands had been killed or wounded. The whole female population would want to lead new and independent lives, and it was only right that their contribution to the war effort should be rewarded with the vote.[19] The notion of 'rewarding' women for their war work became another commonplace theme. Feminists were quick to exploit the argument that women's wartime activity marked a decisive stage in their progress towards emancipation. The flamboyant Marguerite Durand announced the imminent arrival of a new era for women, when a grateful government would show its appreciation of women's patriotism by granting them the suffrage.[20] Feminist leaders in general abandoned their pre-war pacifism once hostilities broke out and devoted themselves to aiding the *patrie*, whether through the Red Cross, or the organisation of charities on behalf of soldiers and refugees, or the recruitment of female labour. In return, they expected recognition, both in the workplace and at the ballot box.

A sizeable body of male opinion accepted their case. Gaston Rageot wrote: 'Among all the novelties which the war, disrupting the old world to create a better one, will provoke, the most striking, perhaps, and the most lasting, will be furnished by the advent of women to national life.'[21] Possibly the most encouraging sign was that the politicians themselves were beginning to look seriously at the 'compensation' argument and seemed to be contemplating the enfranchisement of French women in the immediate aftermath of the war. The socialist deputy Bracke told readers of *L'Humanité* that while none of the pre-war objections to women's suffrage held any validity, women's war work provided definitive refutation of the anti-feminist case.[22] The oldest deputy in the Chamber, Jules Siegfried, declared that the time had surely come to give women the vote to thank them for 'their admirable attitude during the war'.[23] Depositing a female suffrage bill in January 1918, deputy Emile Magniez claimed that 'women have proved that they can be, in almost all spheres, our precious collaborators: let us not treat them as slaves'.[24] Even some deputies on the extreme Right were converted to the introduction of some form of women's suffrage. Maurice Barrès, for instance, proposed that war widows should vote as a way of honouring the glorious dead and perpetuating their influence.[25] Charles Maurras backed votes for women in the pages of *L'Action Française*.[26] The crowning triumph came in May 1919, when, following a historic debate, the Chamber of Deputies voted to enfranchise women on the same terms as men by the overwhleming majority of 329 votes to 95.[27]

It can scarcely be doubted, then, that during and immediately after World War I many contemporaries *anticipated* that major social change was imminent, and that change would be most marked in the matter of relations between the sexes. Nothing less than a social revolution in the position of women was expected. Historians should not lightly disregard contemporary opinion. Neither should they be blinded by it. They do, after all, have the advantage of hindsight. Taking the long-term perspective outlined at the start, we can now see that the social revolution never took place: at best there was a *révolution manquée*, a missed opportunity to bring about lasting change.

Consider, first, the all-important question of women's employment, singled out by contemporaries as the key to women's emancipation. In the short run, the fact that women had proved themelves capable of taking over almost any kind of job during the war in no way guaranteed that they would keep their posts once the war was over. Demobilisation and the return of the *poilus* precipitated widespread unemployment among women workers.[28] The government itself, having enthusiastically recruited women into the labour force for the duration of the war, was equally zealous in exhorting them to return to their hearths after hostilities ended. As an incentive, it offered to pay them a bonus if they complied by 5 December 1918. Under certain conditions, the state was also willing to compensate employers in private industry who made redundancy payments to their female workers. Many employers simply dismissed women workers with no extra compensation. At the end of November 1918 official estimates at the Ministry of Armaments were that, of the 450 000 women employed in the war factories, only one third could expect to be kept on. It was hoped that a third would leave voluntarily, but the other 150 000 faced unemployment. By January 1919 the government was forced to admit that thousands of women had been 'victimised in shocking conditions'. In major cities – Paris, Marseilles, Lyons, Toulouse – unemployed women took to the streets to protest against their dismissal and local prefects expressed their fears of the threat posed to public order. Here was a strange way of 'rewarding' women for their sterling wartime efforts. As one woman told *La Vague*, a pacifist newspaper with strong feminist sympathies: 'My husband has been under the flag for six years. I slogged away during the war. I worked at Citroën's. I sweated blood and lost my youth and health. Made redundant in January, it's dire poverty.'[29]

Demobilisation revealed only too clearly that what had happened during the war was that women, from the point of view of government and the employers, had been mobilised as a reserve army of labour.

From the point of view of the women workers themselves, the most important consideration had been survival. The loss of a family's principal breadwinner was a serious blow: the government's allowance of 1.25 francs a day was inadequate compensation, especially after prices began to rise steeply. In any case, it was paid only to wives and not to mothers, sisters or lovers usually supported by an absent male. In addition, for the first two years of the war, women faced the hardship of unemployment, since production in the 'feminine' sectors such as the clothing industry and textiles was severely cut back. Paris, as the centre of the luxury goods industry, was particularly hard hit. When the opportunity arose to take up jobs in the war factories and elsewhere, housewives, domestic servants and unemployed female workers seized the chance to provide for their families, sometimes earning more than they had ever done before.[30] But it was never understood that the war-time situation would continue indefinitely. Few women regarded war work as a liberating experience. Conditions were frequently intolerable and desperate *ouvrières* turned to trade union leaders such as Merrheim of the Metalworkers Union to ask for their help to reduce excessively long working hours and exploitation at the hands of unscrupulous foremen.[31] Figures for industrial accidents show that women's war work was not only arduous but dangerous. In 1917 there were some 69 606 reported accidents, of which 59 proved fatal, 756 resulted in permanent incapacitation and the vast majority (over 67 000) led to a lay-off of more than four days.[32] The turnover of women war workers in the war factories was extremely high: some did not last a week. In one factory of the fifteenth *arrondissement* in Paris only ten women remained out of several hundred who had started work there only seven or eight months previously.[33] Far from emancipating women workers, war work convinced many that such labour was beyond their endurance. The feminist journalist, Marcelle Capy, writing on the basis of personal experience, claimed that women in munitions factories were asked to do tasks for which they were not equipped by nature. Women's employment in the future, she argued, should be in offices rather than factories.[34]

Capy's prescription was in line with longer-term trends.[35] Contrary to popular belief, the war had not led to exciting new opportunities for women in the world of work. Both the war and the demobilisation involved distortions and disruptions which sometimes obscured the broader pattern, which is best discerned by comparing pre-war figures with the census data of 1921 and 1926. Overall, *fewer* women were employed in industry than in 1906.[36] More than a quarter of a million women disappeared from the textile industry between 1906 and 1921 – a drop of 18 per cent. The clothing industry *shed nearly* 55 000 women workers in the same period, and another 162 000 between 1921 and 1926. Domestic service lost 86 000 women between 1911 and 1921, with another 12 000 following suit over the next five years. At the same time as women were abandoning jobs in the traditional 'feminine' sectors, they began to be taken on in newer industries such as chemicals, electricity, and light engineering, and in the tertiary sector. Thus, in the metal industry in Paris, women made up 14 per cent of the labour force in 1921 whereas they had been less than 6 per cent in 1911. The tertiary sector employed 344 000 women in 1906; 855 000 in 1921; and 1 034 000 in 1936 (by which latter stage it accounted for nearly a quarter of the entire female work force outside of agriculture). The war, therefore did not increase the number of women at work but formed part of a process whereby women were redistributed in the labour force.[37]

The drift away from older occupations into new jobs was clearly visible before 1914. The trend towards the tertiary sector was especially marked and had its roots in pre-war technological change and in the expansion of the bureaucracy. The numbers of state schoolteachers tripled between 1866 and 1936; likewise employees at the Ministry of Posts. Fewer than 410 000 civil servants in 1866 had become more than 600 000 in 1906 and over 900 000 in 1936.[38] Women gained particularly from the invention of the typewriter, the telegraph and the telephone and from the advent of the big department stores and the multiplication of banks. In 1866 they formed only 25 per cent of employees in the commercial sector: by 1911 this had risen to 40 per cent.[39] The feminisation of office work was well under way when World War I broke out. Likewise, at the higher level of the professions, the decisive battles to open up careers for women in, say, medicine and law, had been fought and won before 1914. Julie Chauvin became the first woman to graduate from the Law Faculty of the Sorbonne in 1890, while some 578 female students were registered to read medicine in 1914.[40] Professional women were still a long way from achieving equality with men (in 1929 there were still only a hundred women enrolled at the Paris Bar) but World War I was not a turning point in their stuggle.

Jobs in newer industries or occupations did not in themselves bring a radically new deal for women. The sexual division of labour remained and women workers invariably found themselves in an inferior position *vis-à-vis* their male colleagues. In the munitions factories during the war, women never fully replaced the absent male workers but rather were given the least skilled jobs and obliged to work under the supervision of a male worker. Their deployment depended heavily on the introduction of labour-saving machinery, which created unskilled and semi-skilled tasks to which they could be assigned after the most elementary training. They never had the opportunity to acquire the skills of, say, a male toolmaker, who had to serve a long apprenticeship.[41] In the newer industries women could aspire only to join the ranks of the *ouvriers spécialisés*, or semi-skilled machine operators. Pay differentials reflected their inferior status. The gap between men's and women's wages may have narrowed in the course of the war (in 1916 in the Paris metal industry it was 16 per cent compared to 45 per cent in the pre-war period) but by 1921 it was once again 21 per cent and higher in the provinces (for example, 40 per cent at Toulouse).[42] It should also be said that the trend towards greater mechanisation and the decline of artisanal skill was one which predated World War I and has been identified as an important source of the labour unrest in France in the years before 1914.[43]

A final and crucial point is worth making before leaving the subject of women's employment. This concerns the work of married women. Overall, the proportion of married women in the total female active population not counting agriculture remained remarkably constant at around 20 per cent – indeed the percentage dropped from 20 per cent in 1906 to 18.79 per cent in 1936.[44] After the war, as before it, in their great majority French married women did not enter paid employment outside the home. This was particularly true with regard to middle-class women. The percentage of women in the liberal professions compared to the total of married women in the population was under 1 per cent in 1936.[45] The daughters of the bourgeoisie may have been permitted to work but wives were expected to devote themselves to home and hearth.

The continuing exclusion of married women from the world of work suggests that the revolution in social attitudes forecast for the post-war years was as chimerical as the revolution in job opportunities. The non-appearance of any new deal for women in respect of their lack of civil and political rights points to the same conclusion. Despite all the rhetoric and confident predictions of the war years and their immediate aftermath, married women continued to be denied the right to full legal capacity and all women were denied the right to vote. A few minor changes in the law, such as the temporary right to assume the paternal power (1915) or the right to guardianship of orphans

(1917) did not alter the more important fact that, in the eyes of the law, married women were treated as persons unfit to act in their own right. The Civil Code still obliged wives to be obedient to their husbands, to reside where they chose to live and to recognise their full control over the children. Full legal capacity came only in 1938.[46]

Nor did French women become full-fledged citizens of the Republic. The auspicious vote in the Chamber in 1919 notwithstanding, French women did not receive the right to the suffrage until after World War II. The bill passed by the Chamber was thrown out by the Senate in 1922. Arguably, far from emancipating women, the war was 'actually a setback for the women's suffrage movement in France'.[47] It cut short a campaign which had been building up promisingly on the eve of the war and dispersed its leading figures and organisations. In the words of Hause and Kenney:

> The war also buried women's rights under a host of other problems to which politicians accorded primacy, such as economic recovery or the diplomacy of French security. Such problems created a national mood in which the foremost desire seemed to be a return to the halycon days of a lost *belle époque* rather than to further the transformation of French society.[48]

In general, then, it would appear that there was no close relationship between war and social change in the case of World War I and urban women in the French population. The picture was not entirely negative. Just as French peasant women benefited from higher prices and a higher standard of living, so some working-class women gained from legislation which introduced shorter working hours. Strike action by Parisian dressmakers and other female garment industry workers in 1917 led to the introduction of the *semaine anglaise* (half-day on Saturdays),[49] Further pressure from organised labour helped to secure the eight-hour day, introduced by a law of 23 April 1919.[50] In the case of women domestic workers, possibly the most exploited victims of the entire work force, the government legislated to introduce a minimum wage in 1915.[51] By contrast, many middle-class families were materially worse off after the war, which may have been one reason they looked more favourably on work by their daughters and on girls' secondary education. A law of 1924 provided for equality in the curricula of boys' and girls' lycees and colleges.[52]

For middle-class women, however, the principal change was probably in attitudes rather than in material well-being. Young bourgeois girls, accustomed to visit the war wounded in hospital, began to go around unchaperoned.[53] Fashion accentuated the trend towards greater freedom of movement. [54] Hemlines rose above the ankles, and the new *garçonne* look came into vogue. Moralists and church leaders expressed anxiety about the indecency of female dress. The novelist Marcel Prévost was troubled by the disappearance of the old type of bathing costume, with its long trousers and belted tunic which, he opined, 'would have preserved the chastity of Diana'.[55] Even more worrying for traditionalists was the publication of novels like Victor Margueritte's *The Bachelor Girl* (1922), which explicitly depicted the amorous adventures, both heterosexual and lesbian, as well as the experiments with drugs of a newly liberated middle class girl.[56]

Yet it would be a mistake to identify a certain evolution in social mores with the sexual revolution which alarmist contemporaries made it out to be. Most bourgeois girls, of whom the young Simone de Beauvoir was not untypical, except in her intelligence, still continued to receive a 'traditional' upbringing,[57] while the corner-stone of the double moral standard – the system of state-regulated prostitution – remained firmly in place.[58] The ideology of domesticity was not seriously undermined by the war: on the contrary, if anything, it was strengthened. The loss of 1.3 million men in a nation already obsessed with childlessness and the problem of demographic decline encouraged the state to introduce draconian legislation against birth control in 1920 and against abortion in 1923. As far as the state was concerned, women's essential duty was more than ever to be wives and mothers, giving birth to new citizens to take the place of the 'lost cohorts' of World War I. The future of the 'race' and the security of France as a Great Power were thought to depend on it.

Total war, Arthur Marwick has written, serves as a 'test' of a society. World War I undoubtedly tested the French state and French society to the limit. Yet breaking point was never reached, and the very fact that, in the end, France emerged victorious from the conflict convinced most people – certainly most politicians – that there was no need to tamper with the country's political institutions or social and economic bases. The regime and the social order it represented had been vindicated. In that social order, women were still a long way from emancipation, even as conceived in terms of 'equal rights' without saying anything about 'autonomy. The case of French women and World War I demonstrates that total war had failed to generate significant social change.

Notes

1. A. Marwick, *War and Social Change in the Twentieth Century* (London, 1974.)
2. cf J. Williams, *The Home Fronts. Britain, France and Germany 1914–1918* (London, 1972), p. v: S Verdeau, *L'accession des femmes aux fonctions publiques* (Law thesis, Toulouse, 1942) p. 36.
3. S. G. Bell and K. M. Offen, *Women, the Family and Freedom: the Debate in Documents*, 2 vols (Stanford, 1983) is an excellent introduction to the debate on the 'Woman question' since the late eighteenth century.
4. Y. Lequin (ed.), *Histoire des Français XIXᵉ–XXᵉ siècles, vol. II, La Société* (Paris, 1983) p. 124.
5. M. Segalen, *Love and Power in the Peasant Family* (Oxford, 1983) pp. 95 and 43.
6. Ibid., p. 174.
7. See J. F. McMillan, *Housewife or Harlot: The Place of Women in French Society 1870–1940* (Brighton, 1981), pt II, for the statistical information which follows. See also M. Dubesset *et. al.*, 'Les munitionettes de la Seine' in P. Fridenson (ed.), *1914–1918: L'Autre Front* (Paris, 1977).
8. L. Gayraud, 'L'oeuvre féminine et le féminisme', *La Revue Hebdomadaire*, 22 July 1916, pp. 525–40.
9. J. Misme, 'La guerre et le rôle des femmes', *La Revue de Paris*, 1 November 1916.
10. C. Duplomb, 'L'emploi de la femme dans les usines', *La Renaissance Politique, Littéraire et Artistique*, August 1917.
11. M. Gabelle, 'La place de la femme française après la guerre', *La Renaissance Politique, Littéraire et Artistique*, 17 February 1917.
12. L. Abensour, *Histoire générale du féminisme: des origines à nos jours* (1921) p. 310.
13. J. Barthélemy, *Le vote des femmes* (1920) preface, p. v.
14. H. Robert, 'La femme et la guerre', *La Revue*, May 1917, pp. 243–57.
15. T. d'Ulmès, 'Les Femmes et l'action nationale', *La Revue Hebdomadaire*, 7 August 1915, pp. 73–83.
16. H. Spont, *La femme et la guerre* (Paris, 1916).
17. H. Joly, 'De l'extension du travail des femmes après la guerre', *Le Correspondant*, 10 January 1917, pp. 3–34.
18. F. Lepelletier, 'La situation de la femme au lendemain de la guerre', *La Réforme Sociale*, March 1919, pp. 180–192.
19. F. Masson, 'Les femmes pendant et après la guerre' *La Revue Hebdomadaire*, 3 May 1917.
20. *L'Oeuvre*, 2 February 1916.
21. G. Rageot, *La Française dans la guerre* (n.d.), p. 3.
22. Bracke, 'Le suffrage des femmes', *L'Humanité*, 23 June 1917.
23. *Journal Officiel* (Chambre) séance 8 May 1919.
24. Quoted by S. Grinberg, *Histoire du mouvement suffragiste depuis 1848* (Paris, 1926) p. 113.
25. J. Barthélemy, *Le vote des femmes*, p. 131.

26. S. C. Hause and A. R. Kenney, *Women's Suffrage and Social Politics in the French Third Republic* (Princeton, 1984) p. 222

27. *Journal Officiel* (Chambre) séance 20 May 1919.

28. What follows is based on Archives Nationales (AN) F7 13356 (3): Licenciement des ouvrières de guerre.

29. *La Vague*, 1 May 1919.

30. McMillan, *Housewife or Harlot*, pp. 132–3.

31. Ibid., pp. 136–7.

32. Ibid., p. 138.

33. Ibid., p. 137.

34. M. Dubesset, F. Thébaud and C. Vincent, *Quand les femmes entrent à l'usine* (Maîtrise, Paris 7, 1973–4) 2 vols., p. 57.

35. These may be seen in J. Daric, *L'activité professionnelle des femmes en France* (Institut National d'Etudes Démographiques, cahier no. 5, 1947).

36. A. Vallentin, 'L'emploi des femmes depuis la guerre', *Revue Internationale du Travail*, April 1932, pp. 506–21.

37. McMillan, *Housewife or Harlot*, pp. 157–8.

38. Figures from Lequin (ed.) vol. II, p. 329.

39. M. Guilbert, 'L'évolution des effectifs du travail féminin en France depuis 1866', *Revue Française du Travail*, September 1947, pp. 764ff.

40. E. Charrier, *L'évolution intellectuelle féminine* (1931).

41. Dubesset *et al*, p. 73ff.

42. M. Guilbert, *Les fonctions des femmes dans l'industrie* (1966) p. 63.

43. cf M. Hanagan, *The Logic of Solidarity: Artisans and Industrial Workers in Three French Towns 1871–1914* (Urbana, Illinois, 1980).

44. J. Daric, *L'activité professionnelle*, p. 44.

45. Ibid., p. 39.

46. M. Ancel, *Traité de la capacité civile de la femme mariée d'après la loi du 18 février 1938* (1938).

47. Hause and Kenney, *Women's Suffrage*, p. 202.

48. Ibid., p. 203.

49. J. F. McMillan, *Housewife or Harlot*, p. 146ff.

50. See G. Cross, '*Les trois huits:* Labor Movements, International Reform and the Origins of the eight Hour Day 1919–1924', *French Historical Studies*, XIV, Fall 1985, pp. 240–68.

51. J. F. McMillan, *Housewife or Harlot*, pp. 140–1.

52. Ibid., p. 124.

53. This practice generated a good deal of literary attention. See M. Prévost, *Nouvelles letres à Françoise ou la jeune fille d'après-guerre* (1925).

54. F. Boucher, *A History of Costume in the West* (1967).

55. Prévost, *Nouvelles lettres*, p. 37.

56. A.-M. Sohn, 'La Garçonne face à l'opinion publique: type littéraire ou type social des années 20', *Le Mouvement Social*, no. 80, 1972, pp. 13–27.

57. S. de Beauvoir, *Mémoires d'une jeune fille rangée* (Paris, 1958).

58. J. F. McMillan, *Housewife or Harlot*, pp. 174ff.

2 World War I and the Working Class in Britain
Alastair Reid

I

There can be no reasonable doubt that twentieth-century total wars had a significant impact on the domestic populations of the countries involved. Most obviously there was the removal of millions of young men into the army, there was also a major re-orientation of production towards war industries and this had a major impact on employment and consumption, and finally, in most of the combatant nations, there were substantial restrictions on everyday life brought about by shortages and government controls. Similarly, it should be obvious that the intensity of the impact of these pressures would have varied between nations: depending above all on whether they were defeated, invaded, or both. Thus there was a dramatic contrast between Britain and Belgium during World War I, with the latter experiencing drastic declines in living standards and an increase in death rates among non-combatant age groups of up to 60 per cent. Equally there was a striking contrast between Britain and Germany in World War I as the British stranglehold over sea-borne trade gradually brought the German economy to its knees.[1] Since Britain was not invaded and came out on the victorious side, it would seem likely that her domestic population suffered much less during World War I than that in most continental nations. Indeed, Arthur Marwick's pioneering work on the subject in the early 1960s showed quite clearly that the war was connected, paradoxically, with some significant *improvements* in domestic life in Britain. As a result of the economic, social and political responses demanded by the challenge of a total war, Marwick argued that 'War without itself creating anything, can be an instrument of social change.'[2] Not so much that war would bring about fundamentally new developments as that it could speed up and intensify existing trends, especially in the case of a country so stable and slow-moving as Britain has proved to be in the twentieth century.

Given the current context of widespread gloom about the possibility of a Third World War, this guardedly optimistic, or at least non-pessimistic, view of the impact of war on society bears being re-stated once more. Indeed, it has recently been underlined in an authoritative demographic study by Jay Winter which shows conclusively that death rates among the civilian population in Britain between 1914 and 1918 were either static or fell by several percentage points, and Winter argues convincingly that this was a result of general increases in domestic levels of consumption rather than more specific improvements in health care as such.[3] This paper will therefore review some of the main themes opened up by Professor Marwick's work on the First World War and British society in the light of recent research on war-time social conditions, and then go on to indicate the direction in which our understanding of the problems might best be developed.

II

One of the most striking general themes in the recent research on the impact of World War I on social life in Britain is that it indicates that there was far less qualitative change in social relations than has often been thought. It is a sort of loose, common-sense assumption which still turns up in broad surveys of labour and social history that the working classes became more homogeneous during the war as a result of reduction in skill levels and a narrowing of differentials in wage rates between skilled and unskilled workers. Similarly, it is often assumed that the war, by drawing large numbers of women into manufacturing industry for the first time, had a 'liberating' effect on their experience and attitudes, encouraging collective organisation and wider political awareness.[4] From this point of view, the striking changes which occurred in Britain immediately after the war, for example, the extension of the vote to women in 1918 and the Labour Party's rise in influence around a new commitment to socialism in its 1918 constitution, could be seen as the natural political fruition of an underlying transformation of social relationships. As a result of this loose correlation, the findings of admittedly rather detailed research on the wages and working conditions of British men and women during the war can be of considerable importance in reshaping our views of broader social and political processes.

As far as women were concerned, both the increase in, and the nature of, their participation in the labour market has been considerably exaggerated by over-reliance on contemporary propaganda. The government during the war was keen to encourage women to go to work and keen to look highly efficient in the face of a national crisis, so it greatly exaggerated the range of tasks on which significant numbers of women were employed. Equally, feminist campaigners at the end of the war had a strong interest in maintaining this image as a way of making the maximum claims for continued and extended employment of women, especially in the more highly skilled occupations.

In fact, before 1914, over two million women had already worked in substantial numbers outside the home, not only in domestic service in other people's homes, but also in manufacturing industry, above all textiles and clothing. Thus the war did not see a dramatic explosion in women's employment, and the maximum overall increase was only slightly over one million, or 50 per cent. In fact, given the sharp contraction at the end of the war, the net effect was a small decline in the percentage of women going out to work, from 35 per cent in 1911 to 34 per cent in 1921. The extent to which women were employed as direct substitutes for men in manufacturing industry has also been exaggerated. The overall growth of female employment in the loosely-defined 'munitions' industries grew during the war by four times, to 920 000, but of these only 215 000 (23 per cent) were actually doing men's work. Thus it was as if the women who had already been employed in these industries before the war had been upgraded to men's jobs and the new influx during the war had replaced and expanded the already existing female sector of the industries. Indeed, this is probably exactly what happened, certainly the largest area of women's employment in munitions was the filling of shells with explosives in specially constructed war-time shell shops. Meanwhile, areas of female employment outside manufacturing were growing more rapidly, for example, the number of women working in transport grew by seven times to 117 000, and in banking and finance by six times to 63 700. By 1918 female white-collar employment as a whole was over two million, which was not only twice as large as the number employed in 'munitions' but was also the one area of war-time change which was to be permanent.[5]

Thus the net impact of the war was a temporary increase in female unskilled munitions work and a permanent shift in the bulk of women's employment from domestic service to white-collar and service sector employment. Since, in the cases of new war-time manufacturing employment, women workers knew that they were temporary and frequently felt that they were there for patriotic reasons, they were often prepared to tolerate low wages. Moreover in their new areas of permanent employment, the white-collar and service industries, they found themselves once more in poorly organised sectors of the labour market. Thus, though women's trade unionism grew rapidly during the war, this was in the context of a general explosion of unionisation: the net change in the number of women as a percentage of total trade unionists was merely an increase from 10 per cent to 15 per cent.

Given this lack of a qualitative change in women's experiences at work and in the labour market, it will not be surprising that their experiences as wives and mothers remained fairly stable as well. Indeed there is striking evidence that the period of World War I was conected with a significant increase in the rate of marriage in the UK despite male war losses. Thus comparing the pre- and post-war percentages of men and women who were unmarried, we find that these halved from 13 per cent to 7 per cent in the case of men, and from 19 per cent to 10 per cent in the case of women. There are a number of possible reasons for this: the uncertainties of the war and the post-war economic crisis may have encouraged young people to seek security in permanent relationships; more men who might otherwise have been bachelors probably got married – certainly considerably fewer young men emigrated from the UK after 1918; finally the marked decline in female domestic service already indicated above meant that fewer single women were 'living in' and marrying late.[7] Whatever the causes, this clear increase in the number of marriages was accompanied by a barrage of post-war propaganda and some financial encouragements to strengthen the family unit, motivated by the government's desire to rebuild the population. In any case, the vast bulk even of war-time discussion of the kinds of employment which were suitable for women and of ways of improving their working conditions had always been conducted in terms of their primary role as wives and mothers in the national war effort.[8]

III

From what has already been said about women, it is immediately clear that the social experience of most men would also have been more stable than is often implied: they were not confronted either with a massive influx of female labour or with a breakdown in longstanding marital relationships. Moreover, looking in more detail at British industry in war-time from the men's point of view, it soon becomes clear that here too there was more continuity with the pre-war experience than might at first be expected.

As already indicated in the account of women workers, the extent of dilution with female labour in the munitions sectors has been exaggerated, for the bulk of the women involved were employed in clearly demarcated shell shops, either turning out shell cases on repetition lathes or packing them with explosives. Where they did encroach on work which was definitely pre-war men's work this was at most 'semi-skilled' rather than highly skilled, and, after the initial shock of adjustment, even the most craft-conscious shop floor organisers (on the Clyde) saw the fact that they were women as a distinct advantage: it would be easier to identify temporary war-time labour in the industry and eject it after the war was over. In any case, the point of dilution was not to reduce the skills of existing male workers, but rather to release them to jobs where those skills could be more effectively used, in fact to increase their skills and responsibility by making them tool-makers, tool-setters, inspectors and overseers, or sending them into the army technical corps. Even this revised story only covers the position of skilled men in the more heavily diluted engineering industry. In other important sectors of manufacturing there was far less dilution anyway, for example in coal and in iron and steel virtually none, and in shipbuilding only around one tenth as much as in engineering. Here too it was quite clearly on jobs of low skill and usually light physical demands, for example floor sweeping, storeroom checking and painting.[9]

As a result of this continued reliance on highly skilled male labour in the bulk of war-time manufacturing, it would be surprising if pay differentials between skilled and unskilled men had been greatly affected. However, the figures for wage rates do indicate a general narrowing of this differential so it will be necessary to look at a group of rather technical issues in a little more detail.

In the first place, it is certainly true that across-the-board cost-of-living increases were used in order to keep pace with wartime inflation, and that these fixed-sum increases would have amounted to a far greater proportional increase for the less well-paid. This is, in fact, what caused the frequently observed convergence of skilled and unskilled wage rates between 1914 and 1918. Even in the case of this data, though, the reduction of differentials has been exaggerated by focusing on the 14 per cent improvement in engineering, whereas it seem likely that the 7 per cent improvement in shipbuilding and coal was more typical, at least of heavy industry. In the second place there is, of course, a fundamental distinction between wage *rates* (pay by the hour or pay by the unit of output) and actual *earnings* (take-home pay as a result of the number of hours worked or the quantity of items produced). It has often been argued, again on the basis of engineering, that, since skilled workers were being paid by the hour and unskilled workers by the unit of output, in a period of greatly increased output the unskilled would have caught up even more if actual earnings rather than basic rates are considered. This sounds plausible, but was not, in fact, the case. Because skilled labour was so essential to production and was much more scarce than unskilled and semi-skilled labour, all sorts of bonuses and extras were offered to skilled time workers in engineering, culminating in the widespread adoption of piece rates for craftsmen after 1916. Thus closer consideration of the *earnings* improvement among unskilled engineers indicates that it was lower than the wage *rate* improvement, 11 per cent rather than 14 per cent over the course of the war. Moreoever, if we turn to the other industries where skilled workers were even more secure (shipbuilding, iron and steel, and coal) we find that the wage structure operated the other way around, that is, it was the skilled men who were on piece rates and the unskilled who were on time rates. As a result, figures from one Clyde shipyard indicate an actual deterioration of 6 per cent in the relative *earnings* position of unskilled shipbuilding workers between 1914 and 1918.[10]

In looking at the wage differentials of male workers, then, it is clear both that the degree of change in skilled–unskilled relations in engineering has been exaggerated, and that this sector was not representative. In general, there was no major narrowing of the gap between skilled and unskilled workers in Britain during World War I.

IV

If there was so little change in the experience of social relationships for working men and working women during World War I, how are we to explain the important legislative and political changes which occured in its immediate aftermath? Here it seems the answer is that Arthur Marwick was quite right when he drew attention to the importance of the 'military participation ratio'. That is, the larger the proportion of the population which is involved in a national war effort the more likely it is to be accompanied by major social reforms, or, to re-state it in other terms, the further down the social hierarchy this involvement goes the more egalitarian the social consequences are likely to be. Whatever the objections to Stanislav Andreski's original formulation of this idea (that he stressed the military aspects too much, or that his use of the word 'ratio' implies an unwarranted degree of precision) the emphasis on the social and political consequences of mass participation is a valid one.[11] Put in the crudest terms, this is because of the demand for labour: even if that labour was of much the same type and quality as before war broke out the removal of large numbers of young workers into the armed forces and the increased demand for labour in war industries would strengthen the position of the less advantaged and less powerful groups in the nation.

Looking at the case of Britain during World War I, it seems that this happened in three main ways. Firstly, on a straightforward economic level, workers' positions were strengthened as a result of increasing wage rates in an employers' attempt to attract labour, and also as a result of increasing earnings due to higher levels of output, longer hours of work and less frequent spells of unemployment. This is the economic background to the phenomenon of improvements in civilian health in Britain during World War I demonstrated so conclusively by Winter. Secondly, their positions were strengthened on a more indirect institutional level, as low unemployment and higher earnings lead to a marked increase in trade union power, due to the decreased likelihood of blacklegging and the increased ability of prospective members to pay union dues. As we have already noted, this affected women workers as much as (indeed proportionately rather more than) male workers and the net effect was a greatly strengthened trade union movement. This can be seen in terms both of membership and the financial reserves available for strike funds and political purposes. For example, the numbers affiliated to the Trades Union Congress grew from 2 200 000 to 4 500 000 between 1913 and 1918, that is, by just over two times. As an index of a nationwide organisational increase this is really quite striking, especially given the already substantial size of trade unions in the 1900s. For while earlier explosions in union growth, for example that immediately after 1888, had been just as rapid, they began from an incomparably lower starting-point whereas in the 1900s there were already extensive public discussions of the possibility that trade unions were impeding industrial efficiency. Thus thirdly, as well as the direct benefits of union membership and the increased likelihood of improved bargains with employers, British working people also gained during World War I from their greatly increased consultation by the state. In order to prevent disruption and encourage high output, governments became more and more involved in the resolution of industrial disputes, in consultation with labour over war-time changes in production methods and in guarantees to the unions of a return to pre-war practices. This consultation spread from the most careful consideration of local grievances by bodies like the Ministry of Munitions and the Shipyard Labour Department, up to the inclusion in the National Cabinet of three trade union representatives for the first time in 1915. It also led to the creation in 1916 of a special Ministry of Labour with ambitious goals for long-term social reform as well as a brief to keep an eye on the immediate position of labour in the war effort. This process of consultation by the state with the representative bodies of the working classes amounted, in effect, to a new kind of bargaining in which British governments offered large measures of social reform in order to win the co-operation of their working people.[12]

Understanding the impact of World War I on British society in terms of an improved bargaining position for the working classes offers an explanation of why the war had significant social consequences even though it affected the quality of social relationships so little. Moreover it guards against the possibility that the social consequences of 'participation' might be seen as an automatic effect, guiding our attention instead towards the ideas and actions of the various bodies involved in bargaining, towards the possibility of different kinds of bargains, and towards a careful assessment of the relationship between what was offered by war-time governments and what was actually given by way of social reform in the changed context of the post-war period. By allowing us to conceive of the progress of advance as an essentially dynamic one, this emphasis on bargaining allows us to see that the advance could equally well be reversed, as it was to be in Britain after 1918 due to high unemployment, weakened trade unions, and stern cuts in government welfare spending. Consequently the difference in outcomes in the case of World War I and World War II can be rapidly appreciated by considering the level of trade union membership: in both wars membership rose sharply, but after World War I it fell again very rapidly, whereas after World War II it was sustained by a long period of economic prosperity and thus, through bargaining, of more widespread and permanent social reform.

Finally, this emphasis on bargaining between organised bodies within the nation may also highlight the possibility of important differences between the essentially liberal state in Britain and the more authoritarian regimes in Germany and Eastern Europe. We already know that British governments were more successful in mobilising the war economy between 1914 and 1918, both through effective centralisation of administration and through winning the active consent of the mass of the population. But perhaps this very reliance of a liberal state on consent is what brings the 'participation' effect into play at all, and we should not expect to find it in every national case. The effects of total war on social change are also determined by the nature of the political systems involved.

Notes

1. J. Winter, 'Some paradoxes of the Great War' in A. Wall and J. Winter (eds) *The Upheaval of War: Family, Work and Welfare in Europe 1914–1918* (Cambridge, 1988).
2. A. Marwick, *Britain in the Century of Total War: War, Peace and Social Change 1900–1967* (London, 1968) quotation from p. 15. See also A. Marwick, *The Deluge: British Society and the First World War* (London, 1965).
3. J. Winter, *The Great War and the British People* (London, 1985).
4. J. Hinton, *Labour and Socialism: A History of the British Labour Movement 1867–1974* (Brighton, 1983) pp. 96–7; J. E. Cronin, *Labour and Society in Britain 1918–1979* (London, 1984) p. 23; and for a more recent full-length study, see Bernard Waites, *A Class Society at War: Britain 1914–1918* (Leamington Spa, 1987).
5. Marwick, *Century of Total War*, pp. 105–106; D. Thom, 'Women's employment in Brtain during the First World War' in Wall and Winter (eds) *Upheaval of War*.
6. Thom, 'Women's employment'.
7. Winter, *Great War*, pp. 255–66.
8. G. Braybon, *Women Workers in the First World War: the British Experience* (London, 1981) pp. 112–53.
9. A. J. Reid, 'Dilution, trade unionism and the state in Britain during the First World War' in S. Tolliday and J. Zeitlin (eds) *Shop Floor Bargaining and the State: Historical and Comparative Perspectives* (Cambridge, 1985) pp. 46–74; H. A. Clegg, *A History of British Trade Unions since 1889, Vol. II 1911–1933* (Oxford, 1985) pp. 138–41.
10. A. J. Reid, 'The impact of the First World War on British workers' in Wall and Winter (eds) *Upheaval of War* (forthcoming); Clegg, *History of British Trade Unions, II*, pp. 148–9.
11. S. Andreski, *Military Organisation and Society* (London, 1954). For criticisms see P. Abrams, 'The failure of social reform: 1918–1920', *Past and Present*, 24 (1963) pp. 43–64; and A Marwick, *War and Social Change in the Twentieth Century* (London, 1974) p. 223.
12. Marwick, *War and Social Change*, pp. 73–5; Reid, 'Dilution, trade unionism and the state' and 'Impact of the First World War'.

3 The Social Consequences of World War I: The Case of Germany
Wolfgang J. Mommsen

World War I had been fought by all belligerents with the utmost vigour and, as the fighting continued without an end in sight, all available human and material resources were mobilised in order to maintain the war effort. It is no easy task to assess its consequences. Not only the losers but also the victors found themselves at the end of the war in a state of utter exhaustion, and their economies were in considerable disarray. Admittedly, the destruction by enemy action was, with the exception of France and Belgium, limited, at any rate if compared with the Thirty Years War or World War II. Yet things were never again to be the same as they had been before 1914. In three European countries, the governmental systems collapsed entirely – in Czarist Russia, in Austria–Hungary, and in what was still Imperial Germany – and reconstruction proved if not impossible, at least a long-drawn-out affair. The German Revolution which broke out early in November 1919, even before the armistice had been signed, was in the first place a rebellion against the Imperial authorities, in order to put an end to the fighting at any cost. Only in its later stages did it turn into a political and partly a social revolution in which the working-class parties, notably the majority Social Democrats, took the lead. In a painful struggle the Germans eventually managed to halt the revolutionary dynamics and to establish a new democratic order. However, almost from the start the German Republic of Weimar proved an unstable political system, inasmuch as the upper classes and, with a few exceptions, the intelligentsia never accepted the new order of things, but looked backward to Imperial times for their political orientation. They put all the blame for the evils of the day on the political Left which allegedly had stabbed the fighting men in the back, or at any rate on the onerous conditions of the Treaty of Versailles, and in particular on the reparation obligations.

The Germans tended almost completely to overlook the fact that much of the distress in which they found themselves had been the direct consequence of four years of warfare and economic policies bordering on the insane. The economy had been totally geared to increase war production and then to maintain it on a high level, in the face of ever greater shortages of human and material resources of all kinds. The consequences after the war were obvious. Gross distortions in the economy, an altogether inflated heavy industry sector, and galloping inflation were the most obvious consequences.

The war had taken a severe toll in human terms. Losses had been high; in absolute numbers higher than in France, though a lower proportion of the total population than in France. In the case of Germany, 2.7 million people lost their lives, or about 4 per cent of the total population in 1914; in addition, one has to take into account about 4 million who were wounded or invalidated by war action and had to be cared for permanently at the expense of the public. To put these figures in perspective, about 41 per cent of those mobilised, certainly a substantial proportion, were either killed or wounded in the war. These figures do not of course measure up to the degree of human misery and sorrow which was caused by the permanent impairment of life chances for many and the losses of human live.

It goes without saying that the material losses incurred as a consequence of the war were enormous, if measured in quantitative terms. It is difficult, if not impossible to be precise on this point, but the war resulted in a substantial diminishing of national wealth; it has been estimated that as a consequence of World War I about 35 per cent of national wealth was annihilated either directly or indirectly. On top of this came the heavy financial burden of reparations and last but not least the financial obligations to the war invalids, and the descendants of soldiers who had lost their lives in the war.[1]

Things had been made worse by the fact that in Germany the war had been financed largely, if not exclusively, by public loans for which no security had been allotted. Only a very limited proportion of the war costs were paid for directly via increased taxation. Most of them were financed by printing money, and by backing this up with public loans, thereby putting the bill on the shoulders of future generations. The public had been incited by nationalist propaganda to put all their savings into these war bonds which it was hoped would then be paid back in full with a handsome profit in interest after the war, on the assumption that after victory the enemies would have to foot the bill. The gigantic mountain of debts which accumulated during the war – by the end of 1918 it amounted to 150.7 billion Mk; including the debt which had already been in existence before 1914. At the end of the fiscal year 1918/19 Imperial Germany had an accumulated debt of 156.1 billion Mk, 40 per cent in short-term loans.[2] This had been associated with a spectacular increase of money in actual circulation. Initially the inflationary effect had been limited, largely thanks to the increasing scarcity of goods of all kinds. For the time being few people were concerned about this problem. Nonetheless it was a potential threat for the whole social fabric. Prices had risen during the war by about 250 per cent,[3] and even though this was small beer compared with what was yet to come it caused severe distortions in the economy and the social fabric. To some degree inflation masked the social and economic damage which the war economy had inflicted on German society; for the time being the public was not yet aware of the full degree of impoverishment of society caused by the war. As long as the German treasury paid the interest on the war bonds though at the price of an ever higher accumulation of the public debt, few, if any, people realised that the war bonds were no longer worth much, and that most of their savings had in fact evaporated into nothing.

Wars are usually considered as periods of accelerated change, if not as birth-places for new social formations. Certainly World War I had a far-reaching impact on the social fabric in Germany, even though in the end the forces of continuity proved stronger than those of change. However, in socio-economic terms the exigencies of the war appear not to have initiated anything altogether new; rather they resulted in a considerable acceleration of those processes of change in economy and society which had already been under way for a considerable time, but which so far had been moderated by a variety of political and economic factors which under the conditions of the war lost their momentum.

The war situation changed the general framework under which the German economy had been operating in the last decades dramatically; overnight it ceased to be primarily an export-orientated economy. As a result of the Allied blockade Imperial Germany lost most of its former overseas markets, and it was, with certain exceptions, increasingly cut off from supplies from overseas countries. However, to some degree this could be made up by an intensification of trade with European Neutrals, in particular Sweden, and Norway. In turn this necessitated an intensification of the production of consumer goods destined for these countries in order to earn the currency for the urgently needed imports of raw materials. Notwithstanding this fact a fundamental restructuring of the economy had become unavoidable; the formerly strong export-oriented economy had now to be geared to the production of war materials, and to some degree to developing substitutes for scarce raw materials like, for instance, nitrogen. The details of the restructuring which was largely implemented on the initiative of industry itself, need not concern us here. It was the shortages of all sorts of goods and the increasingly short supply of raw materials which necessitated a far-reaching reorganisation of German war industries. While those industries producing war materials experienced a substantial expansion, the consumer goods industries were cut to size, either through reduced supply of raw materials and/or energy, or, in quite a few cases, by enforced closure for the period of the war, even though the owners were compensated handsomely. The main result was a significant shift in favour of big business at the expense of the smaller producers of all sorts, and, notably the artisanate which in Imperial Germany had always been proud of its autonomy and whose contribution to national wealth was still significant.

The statistics indicate these changes in a quite clear, though perhaps rather crude way as shown in Table 3.1. This shift in the structure of industry necessitated a considerable redistribution of the work force also. The figures indicate, as Jürgen Kocka rightly points out, a shift to heavy industry and in particular to the chemical industry, to the disadvantage, of the consumer goods industries and the artisanate.[4] Admittedly the predominance of heavy industry had already been before 1914 a typical feature of the German economy, but in the last

TABLE 3.1 Positive and negative rates of growth in various industries, 1914–18

	%
Chemical industries	+170
Mechanical engineering and electrical industries	+49
Timber industries	+13
Metal fabrication	+8
Mining	-5
Stone and clay	-58
Textile industries	-58
Building construction	-59
Retailing	-32
Printing trades	-31
Food industries	-24
Leather industries	-17
Paper industries	-20

decade before the war there had been a closing of the gap between the two sectors which now widened again. Presumably the exigencies of the war did not quite create a situation like the one which emerged in Italy, where heavy industry which had been overexpanded suffered a severe crisis right after the war, but perhaps it is fair to say that the overcapacity in heavy industry was a substantial liability for the Weimar Republic in the years to come. In general it may be said that the war economy strengthened the trend toward larger units of production, at the expense of the small producer, who usually had no say at all in the *Kriegsrohstoffgesellschaften* (which in fact largely controlled the *economy*). Likewise the agricultural sector lost further terrain toward industry and trade, although during the war this was masked by a spectacular rise in prices for agricultural products and therefore relatively high profits in agriculture. The rather clumsy attempts at controlling agricultural production, and in particular the marketing of all agricultural products, did little to alter this situation; they only succeeded in infuriating the rural population over bureaucratic interference with their activities.

It is very difficult, however, to draw from these observations plausible conclusions about the social consequences of the restructuring of the economy necessitated by the war effort. Individual industries and trades were affected by these measures in markedly different degrees, and for the fortunes of a particular business the question of whether business activities justified exemption of the owner or the manager from military service was often far more important than economic issues. In later years the military authorities in charge of procurement of military goods of all sorts began to take greater care in placing orders with small producers and artisans, in order to fend off widespread criticism about the unfair consequences of the administrative interference with the economy. Accordingly there was no uniform policy of favouring the big rather than the small entrepreneur, but the general trend certainly pointed in this direction. Even so it will have to be assumed that big business did rather better than the rest of the economy during the war, and indeed the profits in the iron and steel and chemical industries were substantially higher than the average, as is indicated by the development of dividends shown in Table 3.2.

Not surprisingly, contemporaries were already complaining bitterly about the new class of war profiteers which allegedly drew high profits from war production while the masses of the population suffered from overlong working hours, malnutrition and the shortage of consumer

Table 3.2   Dividends in iron and steel and chemical industries

	Iron and steel	Chemical industry	General
1013–14	8.33 Mk	5.94 Mk	7,96 Mk
1914–15	5.69	5.43	5.00
1915–16	10.00	9.69	9.90
1916–17	14.58	11.81	6.52
1917–18	9.60	10.88	5.41

goods of all sorts. Somewhat belatedly attempts were undertaken to subject war profits to special taxes, but their effectiveness was always rather doubtful. It would appear that the war made a fairly small class of owners of capital considerably richer, at least at first sight, while the masses of the population were subjected to increasing impoverishment. This is at any rate the conclusion at which Kocka arrives in his Study *'Klassengesellschaft im Krieg'*: '[. . .] it would seem that, apart from the early adaptation crisis and the months of collapse in 1918, the War was not unprofitable for the large industrial enterprises generally' ('[. . .] *dann scheint sich anzudeuten, daß der Krieg, abgesehen von der anfänglichen Anpassungskrise und den Monaten des Zusammenbruchs für die großen Industrieunternehmungen insgesamt nicht unprofitabel war'*).[5]

However, even this rather cautious assessment is perhaps not necessarily correct in view of the general development of prices. It must be realised that during the war at least dividends, if not profits, lagged far behind the development of prices. From 1914 to 1919 wholesale trade prices rose, starting in 1913 from a base of 100, from 106 in 1914 to 415 in 1919; that is to say, a rise of about 300 per cent. There were certainly many who made personal fortunes by a skilful combination of the exploitation of war-time opportunities and tax evasion, but on the whole it will have to be said that everybody lost out. Rather one should ask, how much they lost, and which groups lost more and which proportionately less. However, the different degrees by which the various sections of the population were affected by the general process of impoverishment during the war is a matter of considerable dispute.

Jürgen Kocka has argued that during the First World War German society came considerably closer to being a class society, in the classic meaning of this term.[6] He contends that the war resulted in a considerable intensification of class divisions, given the falling trend of real wages on the one hand, and the relatively high profits of the war

industries on the other. He assumes that the employers operating in
these industries (he assesses there were about 120 000 of them) must
have experienced a considerable improvement in their economic
position. Certainly they belonged to the winners, though only in
relative terms, whereas the working class definitely belonged to the
losers. More importantly, Kocka argues that the middle classes were
polarised under the impact of the war economy. The new middle class
– that is, by and large the white-collar workers – suffered a
considerable loss in real income; moreover, its formerly relatively
elevated position vis-à-vis the bulk of the working classes was
gradually eroded. To put it in other words, the white-collar workers
were proletarianised and politically radicalised. The old middle class,
in particular the higher civil servants, the smaller entrepreneurs and
the rentiers, also incurred severe losses, but, according to Kocka, in
spite of this they opted for the entrepreneurial camp rather than for the
working class, as they strongly objected to *Staatssozialismus* and
governmental controls of the economy. Hence, in his view, the
cleavage between the entrepreneurial class and the working class
became more and more marked during the course of the war, a fact
which had important consequences for the socio-political orientation
of the middle classes in Germany after the war.

While I agree with Kocka that the war resulted in significant shifts in
the social stratification and the mental orientation of the German
people, I doubt whether the dichotomous class model introduced by
him, though only as a yardstick not as a substantive theory, is
particularly suitable for describing the complex processes of social
change which took place during the war.[7]

Key importance in this respect will have to be alloted to the
assessment of the situation of the working classes under the conditions
of the war economy. There is no doubt at all that nominal wages of
both skilled and unskilled workers rose substantially during the war,
except in the first months after the outbreak of the war when there was
considerable unrest in the economy. Perhaps the most striking feature
was the steep rise in the employment of female labour. In great
numbers the women took over the jobs vacated by their husbands and
sons, and wage differentials between male and female employees
narrowed a great deal. Much the same is true with regard to the wage
differentials between skilled and unskilled labour, though the
aggregate data do not take into account the fact that, as highly skilled
labour had become scarce indeed, many highly skilled jobs had to be
done by less qualified workers whose wages nonetheless rose

accordingly. For these reasons it is perhaps not surprising to find that the status of semi- and unskilled labour improved, whereas the status of highly skilled labour, which hitherto had enjoyed a relatively elevated status compared with the bulk of the workforce, declined, and, that accordingly there was a trend towards a greater degree of homogeneity of the economic situation of the workers. This should have worked in favour of a greater cohesion among the working classes. This observation appears to be in line with Kocka's thesis that class dichotomy became more accentuated during the war. However, the relative decline of differentiation within the working classes may largely be due to the relatively high degree of dilution (that is dilution of highly skilled labour with less skilled) practised in industry under war conditions. However, this need not necessarily have resulted in a stronger class consciousness of the workforce as a whole.

It goes without saying that though nominal wage levels were rising, real wage levels of the working class declined considerably, at any rate until 1917. It would appear that from late 1917 onwards the working class succeeded in fending off further significant falls in real wages. However, the statistical evidence available again probably masks the fact that, as money could no longer buy a sufficiency of essential goods, with the black market being the only way out, actual living standards still continued to fall. Numerous accounts of the misery of the working population leave little doubt about this fact, although it cannot be proven statistically on the basis of the aggregate data which are available to us. On the other hand, it would appear that certain groups of highly skilled labour, in particular in the Berlin engineering industries, did enjoy exceptionally high wages; at any rate it had by now become common practice among skilled workers to play off one entrepreneur against the other, and the latter were prepared to raise their wages as labour was scarce and production costs did not really matter much; the authorities were prepared to buy at any price.

It is certainly difficult to arrive at a clear assessment of the position of the working class. I should have thought that since late 1917, in spite of the increasing misery in the industrial conurbations, the income levels and the economic situation of the working class stabilized somewhat, at any rate in relative terms, if compared with the lot of the people in general. It would appear, furthermore, that wage levels were very much dependent upon both location and industrial sector. Hewers and haulers in the Ruhr seem to have failed to maintain their real wage levels from 1917 onward, while unskilled workers in key state factories easily bypassed them. Printers, for instance, before the war one of the most highly paid groups of workers, did comparatively badly. Though, as Bry maintains, differentials between wages in war and peace industries became less marked after 1917, they seem to have been still considerable throughout the whole period.[8] Besides, living costs varied greatly from place to place, and though the authorities tried to compensate for the comparatively high cost of living and the bad supply situation in large cities by paying special bonuses, these differentials certainly could not be ironed out to any appreciable degree by such measures. Given these circumstances, any reliable assessment of the development of real wages is notoriously difficult. The aggregate figures shown in Table 3.3 indicate this trend clearly, though they ought to be interpreted with considerable caution.

Table 3.3   Real wages for Germany and Great Britain, 1914–18 (1914=100)

	Germany	*Great Britain*
1915	96	86
1916	87	80
1917	79	75
1918	77	85

The relative levelling-off of the decline of real wages since 1917, which must be considered significant in view of the dramatically deteriorating levels of nutrition and supply of consumer goods of all sorts, corresponds broadly to events on the political level. In 1916 the German government introduced the so-called Hindenburg Programme, albeit under considerable pressure from the Supreme Headquarters which demanded that the economic war effort be intensified as much as possible. It envisaged the total mobilisation of all human as well as material resources for war production regardless of the economic consequences or the social costs which this would bring, in order to maximise the production of war materials and raise the recruitment levels once again. But this programme could no longer be implemented without the cooperation of the trade unions. So the trade unions were now officially acknowledged as an equal partner of the government in implementing these new stringent regulations in-tended to push the German war effort up to hitherto unknown levels. The unions succeeded in having those stipulations in the new legislation eliminated which restricted the free choice of the employer, that is to say the exploitation of the opportunities of a favourable labour market on the part of the workforce. It had become a widespread practice to change employers frequently in order to enhance one's wages, in particular in the engineering industries. Certainly neither the employers' nor the military authorities' attitude to the trade unions changed in substance; the old distrust of working-class organisations continued to rule labour relations even now. But the first step toward social partnership had been achieved. Henceforth the trade unions had to be consulted and indeed were given substantial influence in all legislation affecting wage and price policies. This certainly must have had a positive effect on the material well-being of the industrial workforce.

However limited the impact of this breakthrough may have been in material terms, it was nonetheless significant. The working class had shown its muscles and emerged as a comparatively strong bargaining group within the economy, whereas most other sections of the population lost ever more ground. Certainly in Imperial Germany the situation never became one of 'organised labour' versus the propertied classes, the professions, the agricultural interest and unorganized wage earners, that is to say the 'two nations' of the twentieth century, as *The Times* put it at the time, commenting on the development of labour relations in Great Britain.[9] But it would appear that industrial labour was certainly no longer the weakest of all social groups. Indeed an analysis of the economic situation of other sections of German society shows that in all probability they fared comparatively far worse than industrial labour.

One of the social groups which suffered the greatest loss of income in real terms was the higher civil servants. Throughout the war their nominal wage levels remained almost constant, and this was tantamount to a reduction of their real incomes by more than half.[10] It is difficult to understand how this could have been possible, and one may safely assume that without partly living from accumulated savings this group would have been unable to manage. Thanks to the way in which increases were given across the board, rather than in percentages, the middle and lower echelons of the civil servants fared somewhat better. But compared with the industrial workers they did rather badly. According to calculations by the *Statistisches Reichsamt*, salaries of the lowest class of civil servants fell to 70 per cent of their pre-war levels (which was probably roughly in line with the decline in average earnings), those of the middle range of civil servants fell to 55 per cent and those of the higher civil servants to 47 per cent. This shows that the middle and higher ranks of civil servants especially, most of them with an academic training of some sort, lost the comfortable social standing which they formerly had enjoyed. The war thus accelerated what may be called a universal trend pointing toward a levelling downward of the professional middle classes.

The other section of society which at least in part experienced a considerable lowering of its socio-economic status under the impact of exigencies of the war economy and the galloping inflation, was the small businessmen and artisans who were neither active in sectors which were important for the war effort nor owned substantial property. These groups had been traditionally particularly proud of their autonomous social status in society, in particular vis-à-vis the working class, but also the industrial entrepreneurs. Certainly those members of the artisanate who were engaged, directly or indirectly, in services or work important for war production, must have fared rather better than the bulk of their colleagues. But it is safe to conclude that all occupations associated with retailing or services to the general consumer lost out to a substantial degree. The general depression of consumer incomes hit the small shop owner at the corner or the publican particularly hard. Here the rules of the marketplace did not apply, or, if so, they operated to their disadvantage. Certainly small businesses did not markedly decline in absolute numbers, as Kocka points out, at least in the long run. But even so the small retailers, publicans and other consumer-oriented trades fared comparatively far worse than the working class, at any rate if their pre-war status is taken into consideration.

Less well researched is the situation in agriculture. Clearly the peasants, and also the landed aristocracy did well under war conditions, given the dramatic rise of prices for all agrarian products and the limited effects of governmental attempts to regulate agrarian production and to set legal limits to prices. Likewise the inflation helped the big landowners to reduce their debts, however indirectly. But all was not well in spite of the relatively favourable market position of agricultural production. There were severe drawbacks also. Recruitment for military service hit the countryside harder than the cities. This aggravated the extreme scarcity of agricultural labour and made it a hard job to produce under war conditions, all the more so as the supply of fertilisers and agricultural machinery was limited which led to a high rate of exhausted soil. The shortage in rural labour could only partly be made up by employing prisoners of war and reducing the amount of land used for agrarian production, together with a partial shift toward pasture instead of grain production.

Furthermore the war economy had negative effects on the relative position of the agricultural sector in the economy if not immediately, certainly in the long run. The tendency of agricultural labour to leave the land and seek more profitable employment in the cities, which had troubled the large landowners already long before the war, was intensified, given the fact that the wages paid by the war industries appeared to be so much higher. Certainly the war accelerated the rising trend of agricultural wages, compared with those in the other sectors, and after the war this trend proved more or less irreversible. The relative prosperity which agricultural producers enjoyed during the war therefore turned out to be detrimental to the economic position of agriculture. This factor contributed to the relative decline of agriculture vis-à-vis the other economic sectors in the 1920s; whereas in 1913 the contribution of agriculture and fisheries to national wealth had been 23.2 per cent, by 1925 it had fallen to 15.7 per cent.[11] The fact that the agricultural sector still employed 30 per cent of the work force demonstrated that agricultural income had clearly declined. These figures indicate that the agricultural situation was not as rosy as it would appear at first sight, in spite of the windfall profits due to extreme shortage of agricultural products during the war.

All in all it can perhaps be said that the war economy did not bring about an entirely new structure of the economy. The expectations in some quarters that the experiments with war 'socialism', that is to say a largely centrally directed economy would be permanent were soon disappointed, and some of the more marked imbalances in the economic system due to the exigencies of the war rapidly disappeared again in the post-war period, as, for instance, the large scale employment of women. Some of the internal shifts in the structure of industry caused by the war, however, were to remain, even though they became less visible, and must be counted among the causes which made it more difficult for German industry, commerce and agriculture alike, to adjust to the post-war conditions which saw a further decline of competitiveness of agriculture and stagnation in international trade relations.

On the whole, however, the impact of war did not so much create new problems, but rather it aggravated existing ones. Certainly the most important aspect was that by the exigencies of the war economy the in any case painful process of adaptation of the social fabric of Imperial Germany to the requirements of a modern industrial system had been greatly accelerated. This was in itself a destabilising factor. For it should be realised that in spite of the spectacular rise of big industry since the 1880s, in Imperial Germany traditionalist structures and mental attitudes still had been dominant in the social fabric and in the economy. Before the war the socio-economic structure of German society had still been strongly influenced by traditionalist forces of various sorts. In this context the artisanate needs to be mentioned in particular. In this context it may be worth while looking once again at the relative positions of the major socio-economic groupings in German society at the end of the war.

The agricultural community had before and during the war managed to maintain its privileged status as a sector protected from the winds of change and overseas competition, even though it had to learn to live with a high measure of governmental interference with its operations. By the end of the war its classic privileged social position collapsed with a bang, and it had to cope without substantial subsidies from the taxpayer, such as it had enjoyed in the past.

Likewise the relatively elevated social status of the upper middle classes, in particular the higher civil servants and the professions, which had been a typical feature of pre-war German society had by 1919 all but collapsed as a result of the relative impoverishment of these groups during the war and the additional factor that many of their savings invested in government war bonds eventually proved to be worth a fraction of their former value. It is a moot question whether it is jusified or not to talk of a partial '*Depossedierung*' of these groups which are conventionally counted as part of 'old' middle classes. Certainly they were the main losers in socio-economic terms. Next to them have to be mentioned those sections of the artisanate and small businessmen who were engaged in retailing and services of all sorts. They certainly also lost much of their former socio-economic status, but again, it may be that the war merely accelerated a process which had been under way anyway for a considerable time.

It would be misleading to say that the working class came out of the war in a relatively good position. Certainly they had been hit hardest by insufficient supplies of food and almost all consumer goods. Certainly they had suffered most under the miserable economic and social conditions prevailing during the war in most industrial centres. The dramatic increase in strike activity by 1917, irrespective of the harsh reprisals to be expected from the military authorities – recruitment of the strike leaders who as skilled workers were as a rule exempted from military service, into the army was the most obvious weapon – indicates the increasing misery in the working-class quarters of the big industrial centres. Discontent among the workers was so widespread, and usually so well-founded, that the unions found it increasingly difficult to object to all strike action, as they had done during the first three years of the war. But it should be noted that these strikes were largely directed against the war policies of the government, not against the employers, though economic factors, usually shortages in essential supplies, often triggered off these strike movements.

The foundation of the Independent Socialist Party (USPD) in 1917 was largely due to fundamental differences in the Socialist camp of whether the strategy of benevolent tolerance vis-à-vis the government of the day was justified or not. In this debate political issues were paramount, notably the rising irritation about the official war aims policy or the procrastination of government and Conservative Party alike over the reform of the Prussian three class suffrage. Lademacher rightly points out that up to the end of the war the radical *Zimmerwalder* group had a very limited following among the German working class, in spite of the increasing misery of the masses of the population. The protest of the working class was primarily directed against the policies of the government and in particular against the Supreme Command, which put all its hopes upon a *Siegfrieden*, which would make large-scale annexations in East and West possible. The social order as such was far less in the firing line than might have been assumed given the widespread adherence to socialist ideas. Not surprisingly, strikes mounted in early 1918 when the failure at the negotiating table at Brest Litovsk to come to terms with Soviet Russia made it crystal clear to everybody that the authorities were still looking for a *Siegfrieden* regardless of the immense suffering of the bulk of the population. The influence of revolutionary propaganda from Russia must be taken into consideration also, but it was clearly of limited importance. The dominant motive was the desire for peace at almost any price and for putting an end to human suffering whatever the consequences might be.

From January 1918 the discontent among industrial labour was growing and proved less and less controllable by the trade union and party officials who still adhered to the policy of loyal support of the German war effort. But it was not yet in any concrete sense revolutionary as such. The thrust of a long series of strikes and protest actions was directed against the governmental system, and against the policies of the Imperial government and, in particular, against the military authorities (who were deeply distrusted in working-class quarters), not against the economic system. The growing resentment among the working class was not only a consequence of increasing misery and disillusion, in part it also reflected a growing feeling that the weight of the working class within the system ought no longer to be discounted. The workers became increasingly conscious of the fact that the smooth working of the war machinery was dependent on their willingness to work. This is corroberated by the fact that by now the authorities tended to react with elasticity against working-class protests rather than with the usual methods of rigorous repression, motivated by fear that they might otherwise trigger off uncontrollable explosions of discontent, although indirect methods, like recruitment of leaders of strikes or known representatives of the extreme left into the army, were still widely used.

However, in spite of increasing discontent and the progressive deterioration of the supply situation the bulk of the workers were still prepared to follow their leaders' loyalist policies. Only on the fringes did syndicalist and extreme Leftist tendencies surface, but those were in numerical terms still insignificant. It may sound paradoxical, but the working class did not necessarily feel that it was locked up in the losers' camp; at least the trade union leaders and the leaders of the Majority Social Democratic Party were convinced that to carry on as before was not only necessary on national grounds but also that thereby full emancipation within the given socio-political order was within reach. All in all, in 1918 the political, as well as the economic bargaining position of the working-class movement was getting stronger, and the leaders knew it.

This explains why the German Revolution of 1918–19 was not a socialist revolution, although political power fell overnight into the lap of the socialist parties almost without their own doing, and why it never became one, however frightening events looked at the time to bourgeois eyes. There was a groundswell of protest among the working classes which was given a particular thrust by those groups of industrial workers who had hitherto not been politically organised and who favoured syndicalist strategies which promised immediate results. It got under way only somewhat belatedly in January and February 1919 and was definitely defeated only in 1920, after the end of the *Ruhrkampf*. This movement had in actual fact little in common with official socialist policies of either Majority Socialist or Communist allegiance.

These protest movements which were motivated by a cluster of vague syndicalist and socialist ideas eventually petered out. In the end the Majority Socialists, aided by the German Democratic Party and the Centre Party, managed to regain control. This can partly be explained on the grounds that during the revolutionary period neither the government nor the employers risked antagonising the workers if at all possible. Demands for higher wages were frequently conceded without much hesitation. Accordingly, the working class was able to regain considerable ground regarding wage levels. In 1919 and 1920 industrial labour recovered a considerable part of the lost ground in real income, apparently at a much faster pace than other social groups, though these gains were largely lost again during the period of high inflation 1921–2.

Moreover, recent research into the German inflation seems to corroborate the observation that during the revolutionary period government and employers alike considered relatively high wage levels and full employment politically essential, and financial policies were conducted accordingly, even at the risk of fuelling inflation even further. Borchardt recently argued that the commencement of the experiment of Weimar had been possible only because the budgets had been financed with inflationary methods.[12] With his essays on the Great Depression and Weimar economic policies Borchardt has initiated a passionate debate on the question of whether or not the wage levels of German workers during the later 1920s were too high to keep German industry competitive.[13] If this argument is true, it would appear that in the last resort this phenomenon could be traced back to the socio-economic consequences of World War I.

However this issue is finally decided, it is certainly clear that it was not so much the polarisation between an impoverished working class and a class of entrepreneurs who had done well during World War I which determined the course of events in Germany after the war, but rather the decline of the traditional middle strata of society who came to put all the blame for their misfortune on the shoulders of the Left. In contrast, the trade union leadership and the entrepreneurs considered the situation in 1918 ripe for joining forces, in order to stabilise the socio-economic system. For the trade unions this appeared to open up a golden opportunity to consolidate the position of influence on the economy which they had gained in the last years of the war, and give it an institutionalized form, namely the famous *Arbeitsgemeinschaft*, founded on 10 November 1918. Whether this was primarily a move on the part of the trade unions to forestall a radical revolution as Borchardt would have it,[14] is a matter of some dispute. Primarily the unions saw it as a move to cash in and establish themselves firmly on the commanding heights of the economy. It is true that this agreement was not honoured by the working classes as the trade union leaders had hoped. During the second stage of the revolution they certainly preferred to pursue their interests by direct action, including

Socialisation, by which they understood, not a centrally-directed economic system with a huge bureaucratic apparatus, but the administration of the big plants by their workers. But this also provides indirect clues that it was not the working class which had lost most ground in socio-economic terms during the war, if compared with their pre-war status.

Instead, the real losers had been the middle classes, and in particular the civil servants, the white-collar workers, and parts of the artisanate which in any case held a somewhat precarious socio-economic middle ground between business and the working classes. The middle classes were also the ones who suffered high indirect losses as they had invested much of their savings in what were now almost worthless government bonds. The weakening of the socio-economic status of these social groups, which are somewhat imprecisely considered as part of the 'old middle class', as a consequence of the war is not easily quantifiable but it is fairly evident. However, the social status of these groups had been subject to a process of gradual erosion anyway, as a consequence of the gradual formation of an advanced industrial society.

The relative increase of the *Lohnquote*, that is to say the proportion of wage earners in relation to the whole of the population, during and after the war is also a significant indicator of this socio-economic process. Whether this should be called '*Depossedierung des alten Mittelstandes*' is a moot question. Perhaps this should rather be called an all too sudden shift toward conditions typical in advanced industrial societies. Due to the speed with which it occured, there was not sufficient time for the social groups most affected to adjust gradually to the new conditions. Accordingly they reacted to the developments with strong resentment and political radicalism.

This in turn explains in part why in Weimar Germany the middle classes were prone to become a prey to anti-Marxist propaganda far more readily than in other European countries. Seen from this vantage point the bitter dispute about the causes of defeat and about the Versailles peace treaty was merely a reflection of the socio-economic predicament of these sections of the middle classes. It goes without saying that their opting for the political Right, and eventually for National Socialism, in a certain manner jeopardised the future of the Weimar Republic. The roots of Fascism should not be ante-dated, but it is obvious that under such conditions Hitler's promises to free Germany from Marxism and also from the alleged excesses of capitalism found a most receptive audience. The same is true for the anti-modernist message of National-Socialist ideology (though ideology should not be confused with actual policies) which promised a return to a society in which the peasantry, the small businessmen, the artisans and the shopkeepers would be relieved of the relentless pressures of competition from big business.

It should also be pointed out that the war economy and the economic processes which were instigated by an altogether distorted market had aggravated the serious imbalances in the economic structure of Imperial Germany. Heavy industry had accumulated substantial overcapacity; furthermore during the war it had not paid much attention to technological innovation and cost effectiveness; consequently its competitiveness had suffered. The chemical industry which had also expanded enormously during the war expected a solution of its problems primarily from cartelisation, which would allow it to control prices in the home market, and perhaps even overseas. The banking system had done comparatively well during the war, and was willing to cooperate with industry in promoting such ventures. The small producers, on the other hand, never recovered from the inroads made by the necessities of the war economy. In 1907 the proportion of the self-employed in industry and handicrafts had been 15.3 per cent. By 1925 it had declined to 10.7 per cent. In trade and transportation the decline in the numbers of the self-employed was even more marked: The percentage of self-employed fell from 29.1 per cent in 1907 to 21.6 per cent in 1925. To be sure, not all of this was a direct consequence of the war, rather the impact of the war merely had accelerated this process.

It can be safely assumed that the imbalances in the economic structure inherited from war conditions added to the problems of Weimar Germany once the comparatively good years from 1924 to 1928 were over and the economic difficulties began. Again, it is no surprise that the entrepreneurs thought that there was only one way out, namely again drastically to curtail the welfare state in order to reduce their labour costs. And when the democratic governments proved unwilling or unable to do so they concluded that authoritarian solutions must be sought, or at any rate ought no longer to be resisted, should they be put forward for other reasons.

Finally the role of agriculture during the 1920s deserves attention in this context. As has already been pointed out the war had been a relatively prosperous period for the agricultural sector. In the post-war era, however, agriculture found itself all of a sudden exposed again to unrestricted international competition. Naturally both the large landowners and the peasantry tended to look back to the happy days when the state had insulated them from overseas competition and granted them tax relief and other benefits, both directly and indirectly. Adjustment proved too hard for them; not surprisingly it was the peasants who were the first to jump on the bandwagon of National Socialism. The landed aristocracy, in its turn, helped to bring together the fatal coalition between the traditional Right and National Socialism which paved Hitler's way to the Chancellorship. Thus one may justifiably conclude that during World War I a cluster of socio-economic factors and mental orientations emerged which later provided a seedbed for extreme nationalism and, eventually, for the rise of National Socialism to power.

Notes

1. These data cf. Marc Ferro, *The Great War 1914–1918* (London, 1973) and for the German case, Gerald Bry, *Wages in Germany* (Princeton, 1960).
2. Gerd Hardach, *Der Erste Weltkrieg 1914–1918* (Munich, 1973) p. 173.
3. According to Gerhard Bry, *Wages in Germany 1871–1945* (Princeton, 1960) p. 209; (the contemporary indices vary slightly, Calver gives 229 per cent, Quente 257 per cent and the *Statistische Reichsamt* 313 per cent).
4. Jürgen Kocka, *Facing Total War, German society 1914–1918* (Leamington Spa, 1984) p. 35–6.
5. Ibid, p. 33. In the German edition *Klassengesellschaft im Krieg. Deutsche Sozialgeschichte 1914–1918*, 2nd edn (Göttingen, 1978) p. 27 Kocka accentuates the class divisions somewhat more strongly as is indicated already in the title directly alluding to class struggle as an essential element of policies during the war.
6. G. Hohorst, J. Kocka and G. A. Ritter, *Sozialgeschichtliches Arbeitsbuch. Materialien zur Statistik des Kaiserreich 1870–1914* (Munich, 1975) p. 83.
7. Ibid, p. 208.
8. Gerhard Bry, *Wages in Germany 1871–1945* (Princeton, 1960) p. 310.
9. Cf. B. B. Gilbert, *British Social Policy 1914–1939* (London, 1970) p. 12.
10. See the figures given by Kocka, *Klassengesellschaft*, p. 74.
11. D. Petzina, W. Abelshauser, A. Faust (eds.), *Sozialgeschichtliches Arbeitsbuch III. Materialien zur Statistik des Deutshen Reiches 1914–1945* (Munich, 1978) p. 82.
12. Knut Borchardt, *Wachstum, Krisen, Handlungsspielräume der*

Wirtschaftspolitik. Studien zur Wirtschaftsgeschichte des 19. and 20. Jahrhunderts (Göttingen, 1982) p. 154.

13. See *Geschichte und Gesellschaft*, Jg. 8, 1982, pp. 415sq., *Geschichte und Gesellschaft*, jg. 9, 1983, pp. 124sq.

14. Borchardt, *Wachstum*, p. 154: 'Der Staat von Weimar beruhte auf der Koalition von Unternehmern und Gewerkschaften, die sich unmittelbar bei Kriegsende zu einer Art Burgfrieden verabredet hatten, um eine befürchtete radikale Revolution zu verhindern'.

15. Roessler, Konrad, *Die Finanzpolitik des Deutschen Reiches im I. Weltkrieg*, Schriften des Instituts für das Spar-, Giro- und Kreditwesen an der Universität Bonn, Bd. 37 (Berlin, 1967), p. 177.

16. Petzina, *Sozialgeschichtliches Arbeitsbuch III*, p. 57.

4 The Social Consequences of World War II for the USSR
Paul Dukes

A text for this chapter may be found in 'Idea for a Universal History with a Cosmopolitan Purpose' by Immanuel Kant. The eighteenth-century Prussian philosopher included in the 'Idea' the observation: 'The problem of establishing a perfect civic constitution is subordinate to the problem of a law-governed *external relationship* with other states, and cannot be solved until the latter is solved.[1] Towards such an end, Kant believed that a considerable contribution could be made by enlightened absolutism of a monarchical variety. It is unlikely that he would have found the same enthusiasm for the latter-day republican-enlightened absolutism introduced by Lenin and the Bolsheviks after the October Revolution of 1917. Moreover, the concept of global class conflict persuaded the new government to reject what they believed to be outdated concepts of the state and of its external relationship. However, by the 1930s, when World War II was arising out of the ashes of the First, little of this ideology remained alive and the practice of diplomacy had resumed a more traditional shape. Nobody in his or her right mind would want to call the Soviet administrative arrangements of 1936 'a perfect civic constitution', and most analysts, both Soviet and Western, would agree, if to varying extents, that the reasons for its failure to achieve perfection were connected with the shortcomings of its principal architect, J. V. Stalin, and other influences, both short-term and long-term, of an internal nature. Nevertheless, Kant's order of priorities retained much of its applicability. During and after World War II as well as before, the great social changes taking place in the Soviet Union were all largely conditioned by 'the problem of a law-governed *external relationship* with other states' to which the great philosopher himself gave such emphasis.

True, the problem remains compounded by the difficulty of establishing boundaries, both actual and metaphorical, between

45

internal and external relationships. After the Russian Revolution, the accompanying World War I and the ensuing Civil War and Intervention were all over, the Soviet successor to the tsarist Empire granted independence to Finland and Poland while finding itself also bereft of the Baltic States and Bessarabia. As a consequence of the Nazi-Soviet Pact of 1939, except for most of Finland and much of Poland, the losses were regained. By 1945, the 1940 frontier became the basic boundary of the Soviet Union, with some further additions. Although Kant enjoyed good relations with the Russian force in temporary occupation of his beloved native city during the Seven Years' War, he would no doubt have been appalled by the more permanent arrival of the Red Army towards the end of World War II and the incorporation of Königsberg in the Russian Soviet Federal Socialist Republic, with from July 1946 a new name no longer in honour of a Prussian King but of the recently deceased former Soviet President M. I. Kalinin. The gradual establishment of Soviet hegemony over much of East and Central Europe meant discomfort for local peoples and difficulties in dealings with governments more remote.

A further impediment to our understanding is the unfamiliarity of post-war Soviet 'political culture' and its impact not only on accessibility of source material but also on difficulty of interpretation. The consequent wide gulf between Soviet and Western analyists, it must be said at the outset, does not consist simply of a Marxist versus a non-Marxist outlook but possesses also elements of a more traditional nature, parochial and xenophobic on both sides. Moreover, while Western analysis of the end of World War II and the arrival of the Cold War has included a movement from orthodoxy to post-revisionism unaccompanied by a Soviet counterpart, there has nevertheless been considerable movement in the account put forward in the Soviet Union. Most obviously this has involved a sweeping reappraisal of the significance of the role of Stalin, for example at the beginning of World War II. He is now charged with grave errors of judgement rather than credited with an adept response of 'active defence'. There has also been a tendency towards incorporating what the Soviet historians call their Great Patriotic War within the more general framework of World War II as a whole, and to integrate the social dimension with the military.

On the other hand, the general propositions put forward in a history of Soviet foreign policy, 1917–1980, published in 1981, would not be entertained in many Western quarters with much seriousness. For example:

The brilliant victories of Soviet arms and the Leninist principles of Soviet foreign policy, its decisive role in liberating mankind from fascism led to a tremendous growth in the moral and political prestige of the USSR and its influence on the international scene.

What was considered 'liberation' by the supporters of the Red Army was considered a new enslavement by others. The very title of one of the book's chapters would immediately arouse widespread derision or outrage: 'The Soviet Union's Struggle for Peace and International Co-operation, against the Imperialist Policy of suppressing the Sovereignty of Nations and forming Military Blocs (1946–1952).' Churchill's Iron Curtain speech at Fulton, Missouri on 5 March 1946 is represented as 'the summons for the creation of an Anglo-US military and political bloc directed against the Soviet Union and other socialist countries and also against the national liberation movement of the oppressed peoples.' (Such peoples, in the Soviet view, were to be found in what came to be known as the Third World.) The 'warmongering' policies of Churchill and those of like mind were nothing less than 'attempts to repeat the policies of Hitler'. For its part, the account continues, the Soviet government set out a clear position in a series of statements and speeches by various spokesmen and in interviews given by the Chairman of the Council of Ministers of the USSR, J. V. Stalin. There were four major proposals:

1. Peaceful coexistence, including peaceful competition between the two social systems despite their ideological differences.
2. Continued co-operation between the countries that had jointly won the war, which would include the expansion of political, economic and cultural relations, and the renunciation of the idea of forming closed blocs and groups directed against other countries.
3. The strengthening of the UN, with opposition to the transformation of the UN into a tool of any power or group of powers, and support for the rule of unanimity among the five permanent members of the Security Council.
4. Withdrawal of the troops of UN members from the territory of other United Nations; general reduction of armaments; the banning of nuclear weapons.

Allegedly, while the USA and Britain maintained troops in many countries in Europe, Asia and Africa, the Soviet Union withdrew its forces while reducing their numbers from about 11.33 millions in 1945 to something over 2.66 millions by 1948. While pressing for the banning of nuclear weapons, the Soviet Union made certain that it would not be defenceless against the A-bomb by developing its own by 1949. However, as the Soviet Union pressed for peaceful co-operation and the normalisation of the international situation:

> The US leaders rejected the Soviet proposals for peaceful development and went ahead with their plans for military and political blocs against the USSR and the People's Democracies, dragging capitalist nations dependent on the USA into the orbit of their adventurist policies. The first stage along this road was the proclamation of the Truman Doctrine.[2]

And so, clearly, we must reiterate the evident impossibility of a convergence between the Western view of the aftermath of World War II and its Soviet counterpart. While much of this impossibility arose from a 'political culture' with distinctive features in process of formation long before 1917, at least a considerable measure arose from the social consequences of the war itself. While none of the major belligerents had an easy war, by the measure of mortality the USA suffered the least onerous burden: about 300 000 killed in the armed forces and virtually no civilians. In mounting order of horror, Britain lost about 300 000 fighting personnel but also up to 100 000 civilians and merchant seamen. France lost 200 000 servicemen, but also 400 000 others either fighting for the Resistance, killed in retaliation or dying in deportation camps. Over 1 million Japanese were killed in battle, about 600 000 died in air raids. Nearly the same number of German civilians met their death in a similar manner, while 4.5 million were killed in battle or died in captivity, over 3 million of them on the Eastern Front. Up to 13 million Chinese, possibly even more, succumbed, less in actual warfare than from starvation and disease. The Soviet Union suffered most of all in numbers: about 6 million killed in battle, about 14 million combatants and civilians murdered. In addition to all these human losses, there was vast material destruction in the Soviet Union unmatched in total anywhere else – about 30 per cent of the national wealth or the equivalent of two Five Year Plans.[3]

Immediately, we must recognise that suffering and deprivation do not by themselves constitute a commanding claim on the attention of historians, or on their sense of objectivity. However, there are other reasons for maintaining that in the European theatre of war, even on a global scale, the Eastern Front had a distinctive nature and special significance. Other simple figures are indicative. Up to 70 per cent of Nazi Germany's army was involved in operations in the Soviet Union: in 1942, for example, there were more than 150 divisions on the Eastern Front, just 4 German along with 11 Italian in North Africa. Moreover, the Soviet forces claimed to have put out of action more than 500 Nazi divisions and 100 divisions of their allies, while the Western forces were accounting for about 175 Nazi and associated divisions. There can, of course, be dispute about the exactness of these statistics and about some aspects of their importance. But the overall implications are unarguable. By far the largest European war was fought on the Eastern Front.[4]

There must also be a recognition of the monstrous nature of the Nazi plans for conducting hostilities and then for instituting a new order at what was confidently expected to be a complete victory. This aspect of the subject has been more neglected than most, but helped to bring the war to a total greater than elsewhere. Operation Barbarossa's barbaric aim – the systematic extermination of 'Jewish-Bolshevism', so that living space might be created for the master race, led to subhuman behaviour on the part of the invading army unmatched in Europe and perhaps in the world. Many of us have heard of the destruction of the French village Oradour, quite a few of us of that of the Czech village Lidice. Meanwhile, approximately 70 000 Soviet villages and 1700 Soviet towns were obliterated from the face of the earth in a manner largely unrecorded in most of our memories. Leaving the more bestial orders aside, let us take just one example from Field-Marshal von Manstein:

> The Jewish-Bolshevist system must be exterminated. . . . In enemy cities, a large part of the population will have to go hungry. Nothing, out of a misguided sense of humanity, may be given to prisoners-of-war or to the population, unless they are in the service of the German Wehrmacht.

About 3 million Soviet prisoners of war were deliberately exterminated, a larger number of civilians.[5]

Of course, on the other side, Soviet treatment of Nazi POWs was harsh in the extreme, while the 'liberation' of Eastern and Central Europe was brought to the local populations in a manner that was less than compromising, to say the least. To understand fully the uncivilised nature of war on the Eastern as opposed to the Western front, we should have to look into the development of relations between Teuton and Slav going back from the second Barbarossa and Nazi invasion of the 1940s to the first Barbarossa and Teutonic crusades of the eleventh and twelfth centuries.

But the sense of history itself was given a tremendous jolt by total war. Vasily Grossman in his epic novel based on the battle of Stalingrad, *Life and Fate*, wrote of 'the distortion of the sense of time during combat . . . one second can stretch out for eternity, and long hours can crumple together.'[6] This disorientation took a leap into a greater dark with the arrival of the atomic bomb, as the end of total war was accompanied by the prospect of a zero-sum recurrence.

And so, although a history called total was cultivated in the aftermath of 1945, especially by Fernand Braudel and others in France, concepts of structure and conjuncture dominating the event could be applied more conveniently to eras when the rhythm of change was slower and its nature less dramatic. From 6 August 1945 onwards, the potential of the event was overwhelming.

To put the point more simply, the severe impact of World War II on the Soviet Union combined with the even more terrible threat of any future conflict to render impossible any return to whatever normality Soviet society had achieved before 1941. As the world moved moved towards a Cold War no less total than its hot predecessor, in certain important respects more so, a programme of reconstruction pure and simple was impossible. In spite of superficial similarities between the 1930s and later 1940s, there was an essential difference between the two periods. We will return to this point in some concluding remarks after a brief discussion of some of the principal changes taking place in 1945 and after.

As we leave for the moment total war, both hot and cold, and the more violent social changes, we will soon see that it is not at all easy to say that other social changes were completely without violence, or at least in some manner, direct or indirect, influenced by it. A good example of the difficulty of making clear distinctions is the decline in importance of the former tsarist imperial capital city, Leningrad (formerly St Petersburg and Petrograd). Through death and evacuation, by 1943 a pre-war population of more than 3 million had been reduced to just over 600 000. By the end of the war, much of the city was mined or damaged. As a former Leningrad planner described it:

Despite the loss of many important functions to Moscow during the 1920s and 1930s, Leningrad had remained a direct competitor to the

Soviet capital in many spheres. The War physically and psychologically destroyed much of the city. Perhaps even more important in the long run, the War's destruction provided an excuse for anti-Leningrad leaders in Moscow . . . to justify the diminution of Leningrad's economic and academic capacity. . . . By not rebuilding secondary economic sectors, . . . central economic planners ensured that Leningrad would lack the kind of economic diversity so necessary for the maintenance of urban distinction. The end result has been that, to a considerable degree, Leningrad never recovered from the impact of World War II.[7]

Indeed, according to Geoffrey Hosking, the government based in Moscow made every effort even to suppress the record of the heroic performance of its rival during the war, closing the Museum of the Defence of Leningrad, arresting its Director and seizing its archives, as well as restricting access to war-time newspaper files and withdrawing from publication documentary collections on the blockade.[8]

While Leningrad gave way to Moscow, Soviet cities in general were on the rise. To some extent, this was a matter of individual choice for those servicemen who survived the war. It was difficult to keep them down on the collective farm now that they had taken Berlin. However, there was also a distinctive element of organised recruitment in the addition of nearly 12 million men and women to the pool of employed labour between 1945 and 1950, the greatest increase since the First Five Year Plan completed in the early 1930s. Needless to say, conditions in the towns were even worse than in the previous period, with cramped accommodation, often in crowded hostels, and short rations, even starvation, along with low-level wages. Consequently, where labour turnover was voluntary, turnover was high, as workers sought a better position. Therefore, compulsion was applied most extensively where conditions were at their most unattractive, such as in remote coalfields.[9]

As before, as well as organised recruitment, there was labour of an even more dragooned nature, both convict and conscript. The number and composition of the convict detachments are difficult to establish. Western estimates vary between as much as 3 and 15 million, and are thought to include large quantities of German and other Axis prisoners of war, along with suspect returned Soviet POWs and elements deemed unreliable from the newly incorporated territories to the west. Convict gangs did much of the reconstruction of roads and railways in the years immediately following the war, and they remained in existence until the death of Stalin in 1953. During roughly the same period, between 1 and 2 million conscripts of heterogeneous origin did similar work in Siberia, the Far East, Caucasus and Black Sea areas as well as in the new western republics.[10]

From the latter areas in particular, there was mobilisation of an equally brutal kind in the shape of mass deportation. Some of this had occurred in the more immediate wake of the Nazi-Soviet Pact of 1939, as approximately 20 million people, Balts, Poles, Belorussians, Ukrainians and Moldavians, were added to the Soviet population. For example, nearly 900 000 Poles were moved eastwards on the eve of the Nazi invasion of 1941, a movement vividly described in K. S. Karol's autobiographical *Solik*.[11] The most notorious cases are those of the Volga Germans, about 400 000 of whom were sent to Siberia or Central Asia by the war's outbreak, and of the Crimean Tatars, along with five small nationalities from the Northern Caucasus (Chechens, Ingushi, Karachai, Balkars and Kalmyks) – about 1 million in all – removed to Kazakhstan and Central Asia as the war was coming towards an end in 1943 and 1944.[12]

Subsequent frontier shifts, especially with Poland, involved millions of persons being displaced, including a substantial number of Jews who left for Palestine and other points beyond Soviet control. While local peoples were often taken from sensitive frontier regions, Russians were moved in. 'Slavs are again settling on this ancestral Slavic soil', declared *Izvestiia* in December 1946, as immigrants travelled to Kaliningrad, and Immanuel Kant, no doubt, turned in his grave.[13]

'Russification' or 'Sovietisation' in the newly acquired (or reunited) areas caused an incalculable amount of discomfort, deprivation and even famine, especially after a widespread drought in the Ukraine and elsewhere in 1946 – cases of cannibalism were not unknown. Collectivisation in the incorporated territories repeated the excesses of 1929 and after, including expropriation of kulaks. On collective farms, both new and old, harsh quotas were imposed on the reduced workforce. The deliveries and payments were severe enough to make a judicious analyst, Alec Nove declare, it was 'as if Stalin was determined to make the peasants pay for the necessary postwar reconstruction'.[14] Like their comrades – often their former neighbours – in the towns, collective farmers were hurt by such state economic policies as the currency reform of December 1947. In order to counter inflation and the black market, ten old roubles were to be exchanged for just one new rouble. Savings of up to 3000 roubles were to be exchanged one for one, with a declining rate for larger sums. In spite of this reform, retail prices of 1950 at the new rate were 86 per cent above those of 1940 at the old, an actual inflation rate for ten years of 860 per cent. Little compensation for the currency reform could be gained from the abolition of rationing decrees in the same month, December 1947, since there was little to buy anyway. And taxation policies, with more than half the state's income accruing from a turnover tax payable by everybody, were far from adhering to the dictum of from each according to his means.[15]

Exploitation of the body was accompanied by control of the mind. During the years after 1945, restrictions on artistic and scientific freedom were more rigid than in the comparatively relaxed 1930s. To put it briefly, total war, both hot and cold, had led to a more complete totalitarianism. Injection of the simple catechism of 'Marxism-Leninism' (actually Stalinism) was increased in dosage, even if there was a continuance of the war-time compromise with the Orthodox Church, in which believers were allowed to take at least some of their old opium. The Soviet (largely Great Russian) patriotism of the early 1940s was retained in the later years of the decade, with new attacks on 'rootless cosmopolitanism' (often a thin disguise for Zionism or even Semitism).

The principal administrator of this regime was Andrei Zhdanov, who gave his name to the years 1946–8, which have become known to history as the *Zhdanovshchina*. Zhdanov himself has been considered by a least one analyst, Werner G. Hahn, to have been a crypto-liberal, at least in Soviet terms.[16] But bestriding Zhdanov and other leading lights (or obscurantists) like an aloof but all-powerful colossus was the diminutive J. V. Stalin. As a biography first published in 1947 put it:

J. V. Stalin is the genius, the leader and teacher of the Party, the great strategist of Socialist revolution, helmsman of the Soviet State and captain of armies. An implacable attitude towards the enemies of Socialism, profound fidelity to principle, a combination of clear revolutionary perspective and clarity of purpose with extraordinary firmness and persistence in pursuit of aims, wise and practical leadership, and constant contact with the masses – such are the characteristic features of Stalin's style. After Lenin, no other leader in the world has been called upon to direct such vast masses of workers and peasants as J. V. Stalin. He has a unique faculty for generalising the creative revolutionary experience of the masses, for seizing upon and developing their initiative, for learning from the masses as well as teaching them, and for leading them forward to victory.

Stalin's whole work is an example of profound theoretical power combined with an unusual breadth and versatility of practical experience in the revolutionary struggle . . .

Everybody is familiar with the cogent and invincible force of Stalin's logic, the crystal clarity of his mind, his iron will, his devotion to the Party, his ardent faith in the people, and love for the people. Everybody is familiar with his modesty, his simplicity of manner, his consideration for the people, and his merciless severity towards enemies of the people. Everybody is familiar with his intolerance of ostentation, of phrasemongers and windbags, of whiners and alarmists . . .

Stalin is the worthy continuer of the cause of Lenin, or as it is said in the Party: Stalin is the Lenin of today.[17]

In fact, as noted by Milovan Djilas in 1948, the Lenin of today was ageing fast, no longer able to keep up with his correspondence as General Secretary of the Communist Party of the Soviet Union (CPSU), even if able to inspire widespread awe and terror while barely lifting a finger.[18] As he reached his three score years and ten in 1949, Stalin was the subject of yet more adulation, but a man who had outlived his time as he achieved his natural span. His talents, which were not all negative, had been over-exercised in the period leading up to 1945, and were soon exhausted afterwards. It is not our purpose to consider the psychopathology of the cult of the individual, but we should note again the symbiotic relationship between the cult and society. In their adulation of the Leader, which to an extent probably larger than usually accepted was genuine, the Soviet peoples were expressing both age-old forms of reverence for authority and a novel apprehension about their future.

Nor must we neglect the support for Stalin coming from a more materialistic source, from the 'new class' also noted by Milovan Djilas. There were a considerable number of members of this 'new class', both in the CPSU and outside the Party, in the ministries and Soviets. As far as the Party in particular was concerned, the membership was mostly 'new' by 1952, the date of the Nineteenth Party Congress. In February 1941, the total membership was approximately 3.9 million. By January 1945, in spite of heavy losses during the war, it had risen to about 5.8 million. The rate of growth then continued, but slowed down: by September 1947, 6.3 million, and by October 1952, just under 6.9 million. Allowing for those dismissed from the Party, a guarded estimate indicates that about 75 per cent of the membership in 1952 had joined since the outbreak of war in June 1941, and that roughly the same percentage was under 45 years of age. While the bulk of the new recruits were of peasant and worker origin, they appear to have risen for the most part to managerial level. The educational level had gone up, too, the percentage of those having completed secondary education having climbed from less than 15 per cent in 1941 to about 20 per cent in 1947. In 1952, nearly 12 per cent had experienced some degree of higher education. To complete this statistical account, we should note one more percentage increase, of women: from just below 15 per cent in 1941 to over 19 per cent in 1952.

The composition of Party high society did not reflect accurately the compostion of the Party as a whole. For example, of the delegates to the Nineteenth Congress in 1952, less than 20 per cent had joined during or after the war. About 36 per cent had joined in the 1920s, and another 36 per cent or so had joined in the 1930s. Promotion rates at the top level had slowed down for men, and had still to rise for women – in 1952, only 2 out of 125 full members of the Central Committee were women.[19]

Here is just one indication of the manner in which, even after a traumatic war in which relationships between the sexes had gone through some important changes, old patterns persisted. At least one analyst has argued:

> the very fact that this devastating war, more costly for Russia in human and economic terms even than the first, produced so few significant changes in the structure or political culture of Soviet society is, in my view, the most eloquent evidence that the society had become restabilized, and its political culture 're-knit', before the outbreak of the war. Evidence of long-term economic and social processes bears this out: the fundamental and dramatic processes of social change – industrialization, urbanization, the creation of the new elites – although they had not entirely run their course, were slowing by the beginning of the 'forties, and had already established the basic patterns and relationships that were to be reconstituted and redefined in the post-war period.[20]

Edward L. Keenan suggests three principal reasons for the entrenchment of traditional elements in the new political culture. First, the heavily centralist Bolshevik Party, for reasons of repression and exile inflicted by the tsarist government and its own predilection for conspiratorial apartness, had little experience of the realities of the early twentieth century. Second, the continuance of social revolution and intra-party strife had eliminated nearly everybody devoted to the creation of a non-traditional political culture. Third and of greatest importance in Keenan's view, the new elite that took shape during the 1930s was of predominantly peasant or proletarian background, and its political culture had therefore emerged from a village political culture whose roots were to be found in the communal structure of medieval peasant society.

The force of Keenan's argument is difficult to resist. Moreover, throughout this essay we have insisted that many aspects of Soviet society during and after World War II can be understood only if a long-term historical perspective is adopted. On the other hand, some of Keenan's particular assertions have a flimsy foundation. For example, the figures presented above concerning the delegates to the Nineteenth Congress in 1952 showed that more than a third had joined the Party in the 1920s in addition to a roughly equal proportion that had joined in the 1930s. And so we cannot by any means be certain that nearly everybody devoted to the creation of a non-traditional political culture had been eliminated. As ever, life at the top of Soviet society was precarious, a struggle for place, power and principle raging under the cover of devotion to the Leader.

More generally, let us recall in conclusion the text from Immanuel Kant and the onset of the Cold War. Some superficial appearances and, indeed, some deeper realities notwithstanding, the external relationships with the USA and the rest of the world quickly became a governing influence on the manner in which the road to communism was resumed. Soviet society as a whole had passed the test of total war, and its apologists could now proclaim again with enthusiasm their belief in the fundamental rightness of the teaching of Marx, Lenin and Stalin.[21] But new hostilities would temper that zeal with anxiety in the late 1940s. As the USSR recovered from the agonies of death and destruction inflicted in the earlier part of the decade, the problem of establishing a perfect civic constitution could not be put on the immediate agenda once again.

Notes

1. Immanuel Kant, 'Idea for a Universal History with a Cosmopolitan Purpose', in Hans Reiss (ed.) *Kant's Political Writings* (Cambridge, 1970) p. 47.

2. B. N. Ponomaryov and others (eds) *History of Soviet Foreign Policy, 1917–1980*, vol. 2 (Moscow, 1981) pp. 124–8.
3. A. J. P. Taylor, *The Second World War: An Illustrated History* (London, 1975) pp. 229–30.
4. Oleg Rzheshevsky, *World War Two: Myths and Realities* (Moscow, 1984) p. 104. The fullest Western account is John Erickson, *Stalin's War with Germany*, 2 vols. (London, 1975, 1983).
5. Alexander Werth, *Russia at War, 1941–1945* (London, 1964) pp. 637–8; Christian Streit, *Keine Kameraden: Die Wehrmacht und die sowjetischen Kriegsgefangenen, 1941–45*, as reviewed by Hans Mommsen, *Bulletin of the German Historical Institute, London*, 1 (1979) pp. 18–19. See also Omer Bartov, *The Eastern Front, 1941–5: German Troops and the Barbarisation of Warfare* (London, 1986).
6. Vasily Grossman, *LIfe and Fate* (London, 1986). pp. 48–9.
7. Edward Bubis and Blair A. Ruble, 'The Impact of World War II on Leningrad', in Susan J. Linz (ed.) *The Impact of World War II on the Soviet Union* (Totowa NJ, 1985) p. 203.
8. Geoffrey Hosking, *A History of the Soviet Union* (London, 1985) p. 314.
9. Sheila Fitzpatrick, 'Postwar Soviet Society: The "Return to Normalcy", 1945–1953' in Linz, *The Impact*, pp. 137–41.
10. Ibid., pp. 141–4.
11. K. S. Karol, *Solik: Life in the Soviet Union, 1939–1946* (London, 1986).
12. See A. M. Nekrich, *The Punished Peoples*, (New York, 1978); Robert Conquest, *The Nation Killers: The Soviet Deportation of Nationalities* (London, 1970).
13. Quoted by Fitzpatrick in Linz, *The Impact*, p. 134.
14. Alex Nove, *An Economic History of the USSR* (London, 1972) p. 298.
15. Ibid., pp. 308–12.
16. Werner G. Hahn, *Postwar Soviet Politics: The Fall of Zhdanov and the Defeat of Moderation, 1946–53* (Ithaca NY, 1982).
17. G. F. Alexandrov et. al., *Joseph Stalin: A Short Biography* (Moscow, 1949) pp. 201–3.
18. M. Djilas, *Conversations with Stalin* (London, 1963) p. 118.
19. L. Schapiro, *The Communist Party of the Soviet Union*, 2nd ed. (London, 1970) pp. 527–32.
20. Edward L. Keenan, 'Muscovite Political Folkways', *The Russian Review*, 45 (1986) pp. 167–8.
21. A moderate statement of such a view is Rudolf Schlesinger, *The Spirit of Post-War Russia: Soviet Ideology, 1917–1946* (London, 1947).

Useful works not directly cited in this chapter include T. Dunmore, *Soviet Politics, 1945–53* (London, 1984) and R. Pethybridge, *A History of Post-War Russia* (London, 1966).

I am grateful to Dr. Robert Service of the School of Slavonic and East European Studies, London, for his helpful comments on this chapter.

5   World War II and Social Change in Germany

Mark Roseman

At first sight, total war would seem likely to have had a greater impact on Germany between 1939 and 1945 than any war on any other nation. Surely the war waged by Germany was the most total ever? Was it not a German, Josef Goebbels, who, alone of all the statesmen involved in World War II, presented a total war not as a necessary evil but as something heroic and desirable: '*Wollt ihr den totalen Krieg?*' And surely the Germans experienced the destructive capacity of modern war as intensively as any people has ever done? Yet if this is so, it is striking how little of the historical research concerned with social change in Germany has concentrated solely on the war years or on the impact of war. The emphasis has been on the Nazi period as a whole; 'fascism' or 'Nazism', rather than 'total war' have been seen as the transformative experience for the German people.[1]

Why is this? One point is, of course, that when democracy re-emerged in West Germany after the war it did so to a society for whom total war was merely one of a series of powerful shocks. Democracy was suspended in Germany not, as in Britain, simply by five or six years of war but twelve years of facism and a further four of occupation. So to understand the new features of post-war society it will not do to look at the war alone. In addition, many German observers, whether explicitly or implicitly, have seen war and war-time measures essentially as a continuation of the Nazis' pre-war policies. In the German context, therefore, analysis of the impact of total war must be accompanied by at least some investigation of the changes wrought by the Nazis before 1939 and by the Occupying powers after 1945. This is a truly massive subject, and one on which a lot of the research remains to be done. In the present contribution, which can do little more than touch on some of the most important issues, attention is focussed on two aspects of German society. One is social policy in a broad sense. It has been frequently argued that total war irrevocably advances the frontiers of state intervention in society and encourages social reforms and social engineering; the question is to what extent and as a result of what factors this applies to Germany both during and after the war. The other aspect is the position of the working class in West German society. If there is one striking contrast between the Weimar and Bonn republics it is the absence in the latter of the tensions and polarisation of the former, the diminution of class-conflict and the disappearance of left and right-wing radicalism. To what extent – that is the question here – were fascism or war responsible for this change?

II

When the war came to Germany in 1939, its impact on Nationalist Socialist policy was rather limited. True, the call-up proceeded relatively quickly and by May 1940 over 4 million men had been called to arms. But in general the outbreak of war did not precipitate major changes in the state's role in society.[2] One reason for this was that many of those features of war-time experience – particularly the mobilisation of society and economy – that were novel in, for example, Britain and the USA had already been implemented or at least prefigured by the six years of Nazi rule prior to 1939. Germany had, as it were, already experienced a rather 'total' peace.

Consider the example of industrial relations. In both World Wars, the advanced industrial nations have felt obliged, with greater or lesser degrees of consultation or coercion, to intervene in the relations between capital and labour. The primary motivation has been to prevent strikes that might endanger vital production and to ensure that wage settlements are in alignment with established economic priorities. In Germany, the state had already arrogated the necessary powers to itself in 1933 and 1934. The unions were forcibly dissolved and state commissioners, '*Treuhänder der Arbeit*', appointed to fix wage levels.

Beyond industrial relations, the 4-Year Plan in 1936 created the machinery and procedures to institute widespread controls over the economy. Although, as we now know, there were many limits to the competence and coherence of the 4-Year Plan organisation, it is a fact that before war broke out in 1939, Germany's occupational structure, investment activity and raw materials allocation had already undergone substantial modification in preparation for the needs of war.[3] Many analysts speak of a 'peace-time war economy'

(*Kriegswirtschaft im Frieden*). Apart from the specific achievements of the 4-Year Plan, there were other signs of a general encroachment of the state economy. Compulsory labour directions were implemented in the 1930s; there was the *Reichsarbeitsdienst* for young men and a compulsory year's work on the land for young women. The result was that the outbreak of war required far fewer new measures than in the democracies – the relationship of state and society had been sufficiently redefined, liberty sufficiently curtailed already.

Many of these changes, particularly the restrictions on group and individual liberty but also, to a certain extent, the organising of economic life were not designed primarily to meet the needs of a future war. It is not in dispute that the Nazis in general and Hitler personally gave military and economic preparations for war high priority; the notion of an eternal struggle between nations was central to Hitler's ideology. And what the advance calculation of military requirements certainly did do was to ensure that those anti-modernist elements of the National Socialist programme which initially hindered rearmament – the support given to the small businessmen and the farmers, for example – were speedily removed. But elsewhere the role of war preparations is less direct. The increasingly intimate co-operation between the state and leading industrialists in planning and controlling the economy manifested (and encouraged) a grander conception which it was intended should outlast any future conflict. With growing clarity, leading industrialists and Nazis promulgated the notion of a highly centralised and organised economy, an authoritarian corporatism, which it was intended should provide a German rival to American-style capitalism.[4] Similarly, the Nazis' attack on the parties, the unions and political liberties (which, of course, went far beyond what the Western Allies deemed necessary for their war effort) was designed to consolidate the Nazis' power in peacetime and to impose the Führer-Prinzip on both politics and the economy. The Nazis certainly hoped and believed that society thus remodelled would be effective at waging war. Nevertheless, the changes implemented by the Nazis were intended to be permanent, creating a new order in peace as well as war.

It is therefore hard, and perhaps also unnecessary, to determine how far the extension of state activity and the mobilising of society and economy before 1939 were a sign that war was already asserting itself in peacetime and how far they manifested other National Socialist goals and ideals. Having said that, there is no doubt that from 1936 onwards the direct impact of the rearmament drive became ever more obvious as armaments and autarky projects absorbed ever greater resources and the occupational structure of the labour force shifted towards war production.

The other key reason for the lack of change in 1939 was that, as most historians agree, Germany waged a far from total war, at least until 1942.[5] In the field of economic mobilisation, from having been so far ahead in 1939, the Nazis were slow to consolidate their control. If the economy prior to 1939 was the 'peace-time war economy', the economy between 1939 and 1942 was just as much the 'war-time peace economy' (*friedensähnliche Kriegswirtschaft*). For example, it was not until the labour registration law of January 1943 that the Nazis laid the basis for total mobilisation of labour – and even then the full potential of the law was never exploited. Similarly, it was not until 1942–3 that the Nazis began to ensure that industry was thoroughly combed for inessential employment. Particularly in the first half of the war (although in fact through out the war years) Germany harnessed its population to the war effort less effectively than Britain or the USA.[6]

The limits to wartime mobilisation can in part be explained by the fact that, for the first two years of the war, Germany pursued a type of campaign brilliantly suited to its state of half-preparedness. The strategy of lightning war was a deliberate attempt to avoid the need for armament in depth. But, as is well known, Germany was not properly prepared even for the *Blitzkrieg*. The three-week campaign against Poland in 1939 completely exhausted the supply of spare parts and key munitions. Germany in 1939 presents the curious picture of a nation in which centralised planning and the reorientation of society and economy to war-time needs was already well advanced and yet one in which basic requirements for sustained military effort were lacking.[7]

Another part of the explanation is that the Nazis were unwilling to impose too many sacrifices on the population. This was already apparent before the outbreak of war when, particularly after 1936, the economy began to overheat and suffered from an ever more acute labour shortage. Despite the absence of trade unions, key labour groups were able, on an individual basis, to exploit their scarcity value and negotiate wage increases, a tendency which the Nazis did not resist, despite the costs involved to the war effort.

Once the war started, the Nazis remained very sensitive to public opinion. During the first two years of the war, a whole series of government measures were attempted which were then withdrawn completely or only very half-heartedly implemented. As late as 1943 moves, for example, to revise piece-work rates in order to stimulate higher productivity were made very half-heartedly.[8] Even when new rates had been determined they were often not implemented. The Nazis' reluctance to upset the established wage structure stemmed from the fear that any change would open a pandora's box of resentment about existing wage differentials. It is perhaps ironic, but certainly comprehensible that Germany's fascist leaders felt less assured of their legitimacy and thus less able to mobilise society than were the democratic governments of the Western Allied powers.

In addition to the nervousness of the Nazis, there was also the fact that the confusing proliferation of competing authorities, special plenipotentaries and powerful interest groups made the regime susceptible to a whole variety of pressures. For example, even before the war, the quest of the DAF (German Labour Front) for power had led it to espouse workers' demands and encourage the drive for higher wages. Business interests found spokesmen at every level and were often able to oppose mobilisation measures. Even when a policy had been decided upon by the body nominally responsible for a particular area, it was perfectly possible for it to be sabotaged by some other organisation.[9]

In the case of the mobilisation of women, these two factors were joined by a third – the reluctance of important sections of Nazi leadership to involve German women – the mothers of today and tomorrow – in the rigours of war production. This reluctance was an amalgam of traditional cosy bourgeois views on women's place at the hearth and a new racist social-eugenic stress on the importance of optimum conditions for reproduction. One result of this ideology was that wives of enlisted men were given a very high income supplement, so that many stayed at home or even left former employment. All later attempts to reduce these supplements so as to encourage female employment failed in the face of ideologically motivated resistance and fear of a deleterious impact on soldiers morale. As a result the number of German women in the economy actually fell between 1939 and 1941 and in 1942 was still lower than in the pre-war period. Whereas in 1943 almost two-thirds of British women were in employment, the equivalent figure for Germany was only 46 per cent.[10]

The regime's reluctance to extend or intensify social and economic mobilisation at home encouraged it to exploit the occupied countries. They were to bear the full brunt of Nazi tyranny in order to protect the German population from the ravages and demands of war. Thanks to the massive confiscation of foodstuffs, manufactured and luxury goods abroad, living standards at home remained remarkable stable until towards the end of the war. After a drop in 1942, rations, for example, did not fall again significantly until the summer of 1944. Even more important than the importation of material resources was the recourse to foreign labour. By August 1944 there were over 7.5 million foreign workers on German soil, making up around one-quarter of all employees. By resorting to conscript labour, the Nazis were able to avoid or defer a whole range of unpleasant measures in relation to the German population such as the diversion of labour from inessential plants, enforced rationalisation and retraining, the mobilisation of women and so on.

The general point is that, for a variety of reasons, war-time social and economic policy relating to the *German* population was very often simply a continuation or a modest extension of peace-time policies. What the war did bring about, however, was the cessation or suspension of a number of social experiments in which the Nazis had been engaged during the 1930s. Not all of the Nazis' social engineering was sacrificed to the war effort; racial policy, as is well known, became more and more radical and there was also the continued reluctance to mobilise women. But, generally, social political goals were shelved for the duration. During the 1930s there had been, for example, various attempts to integrate the working class into the *Volksgemeinschaft*. Employers had been encouraged, particularly by the Nazi labour organisation – the DAF – to improve their social policy provisions. Some employees had been given the chance to become owners of their own homes. Opportunities for upward mobility had been consciously created by the Nazi organisations. The Strength Through Joy movement had given considerable numbers of workers the chance to be tourists for the first time. All sorts of symbolic gestures had been made to indicate that the old class divisions no longer applied in the new Germany, the employers, for example, joining the DAF. But during the war, the DAF, though it continued to suggest possible post-war social reforms, became little more than an adjunct of the Nazis productivity policy. It was no time for '*sozialer Klimbim*'.[11]

As the war drew on, the severity and intensity of the measures taken to sustain the war effort increased. The impetus came from the failure of the Russian campaign in the second half of 1941 which galvanised Hitler and the Nazi leadership to take mobilisation more seriously. Hitler's directive, 'Armaments 1942', which appeared in January of that year, the appointment of Speer as Armaments Minister in February, and the elevation of the Gauleiter Fritz Sauckel to General

Commissioner for Manpower, all indicated and encouraged the change in approach that was taking place. Between May 1941 and 1943, the number of industrial workers called to arms doubled; by mid-1944 40 per cent of the industrial workforce had been enlisted. By then almost half of all German adult males were in the army or had died in combat. In the reorganisation of the economy, the Nazis were much less successful than in the call-up and many of the restraints noted above continued to apply. Nevertheless, such measures as retraining labour for work in the armaments industry met with considerable success. A considerable, although not quantifiable, shift took place in the occupational and qualification structure of the German workforce. From mid-1942 onwards, Sauckel was increasingly effective at preventing undesirable, voluntary labour mobility, while at the same time labour direction increased and in the course of 1942 over a million German workers were transferred to war production. The mobilisation of German women, on the other hand, remained half-hearted and brought only limited results.[12]

These policies were augmented and supported by the expansion of the police state as the strains of total war increased the Nazis' anxieties about their position. State terror became an increasing part of everyday life. By 1944, death sentences were being imposed on 14–16 year olds. Between 1940 and 1943, the annual number of executions increased from 926 to 5336. The Gestapo also took an ever more active role in enforcing discipline at work. In 1942, 7311 workers were arrested by the Gestapo for breaches of labour discipline, but by 1944 the figure had risen to 42 505.[13]

The growing use of terror had yet another rationale. For alongside and sometimes in direct opposition to the mobilisation of society's energies for the war effort, the Nazis were engaged in increasingly radical racist and imperialist policies. The war encouraged such policies in a number of ways. War-time occupation provided, for the first time, the opportunity to create the European empire of which had Hitler had already dreamt in the 1920s. Industry was quick to exploit the opportunities and comprehensive plans were drawn up in 1940–1 for the creation of a closed European economy, dominated by Germany. In the East, the occupation of vast tracts of Russian and East European territory allowed the Nazis to initiate their utopian plans for racial resettlement and the subjugation of the Slavic peoples. The war against the Soviet Union exposed and unleashed that hatred of the Russians that was deeply ingrained in substantial sections of the military elite. The war also forced a new solution to what the Nazis regarded as the Jewish problem. It became impossible to get rid of the Jews through emigration and, in addition, the occupation of Poland presented the Germans with millions of additional Jews to dispose of. Under cover of war and unrestrained, as in the 1930s, by the desire to maintain good-will in the West, competing Nazi agencies tried various means of removing the Jewish element culminating in the extermination camps.[14]

Much of this activity impinged on German society only indirectly, or only on small proportions of it: on those German minorities unlucky enough to be the victims; on the sections of the business, political and administrative elites involved in planning and extending the racial and economic empire; on the SS units charged with dirty work. It is true that most of the millions of German soldiers who at some point or other fought on the Eastern Front had at least some experience or involvement in National-Socialist policies towards Russian citizens, whether prisoners of war or civilians. How could they not: in the months November, December 1941 and January 1942 alone, for example, *half a million* Russian POWs died in German captivity. A British investigation of German soldiers' wallets discovered that they generally contained three categories of photo: mother and girlfriend, pornographic, and atrocities.[15] Yet such experiences, important, shocking or brutalising though they may have been, were usually shortlived episodes and had no systematic character.

The one area of Nazi racial policy which did involve the extended participation of a substantial proportion of the German population was the use of conscript labour. In its scope and social impact, this was unquestionably the most significant innovation in domestic war-time policy. At the beginning of the war, substantial sections of the leadership had been hostile to the use of large numbers of foreign workers on German soil. Some had been concerned about the threat to internal security, others about the implications for national hygiene and racial purity. Yet from the early months of the conflict, labour shortages combined with the resistance to total mobilisation of the German population made pressing the recruitment of foreign labour. Once this had been acknowledged, all those sections of the Nazi leadership that had viewed the use of foreign labour with suspicion now set to work to create the conditions which would avert the ostensible dangers of employing racially inferior foreigners and would remind the German population of its role and responsibility as the racial elite of Europe. As the number of different nationalities amongst the conscript labour grew, the Nazis developed an ever more complex and comprehensive hierarchy of rules which dosed payment, nutrition, freedom, living standards and severity of punishment according to the racial 'calibre' of the group involved and their status as civilians or POWs. German workers were drawn into a series of complex relationships with the forced labour. It was a deliberate aim of the Nazis to make the workers active participants in the regime's racist and imperialist policy, to practice in *Kleinformat* in the factory that racial imperialism which would be enacted on a grand scale in Europe after the war.[16]

In their forced labour policy as in many other of their war-time measures it is evident that the solutions adopted to the problems posed by the war were influenced as much by pre-existent features of the Nazi regime as by any inherent characteristics of total war. The Nazis' imperialist and racial ideology, their ruthlessness but also their insecurity all left an indelible stamp on war-time policy. And after 1945, when the Nazis had fallen, it was the continuities, the specifically National Socialist elements in war-time policy, which left an abiding impression on German and foreign observers alike.

III

Total defeat, when it came, provided the opportunity to create a new society. The war had so drained Germany's military, social and psychological resources that the way was open for the victorious powers to reshape the nation as they wished. This is clearly manifested by Soviet occupation policy which, in the space of a few years, totally reorganised society and economy within its influence. In the Western Zones, however, the underlying trend was restorative. A capitalist democracy was created on the same lines as Weimar. True, the new constitution was more overtly federalistic, most of the major parties had experienced some change in identity and a change of name, and the economy was subjected to a certain amount of decartellisation and reorganisation. Yet there was a great deal of institutional and even personal continuity. In politics and the labour movement, the leaders of the Weimar era returned to their former positions. In industry and administration only a few top Nazis were removed, otherwise there was little change.[17]

The war had little positive influence on economic and social policy in the post-war era. In many Western countries, the close involvement of the state in war-time mobilisation created a precedent for continued involvement in peace-time economic affairs and for a more managed economy generally. In such cases, war-time not only enlightened the state as to the role it might play in the economy but also increased the 'fiscal capacity' of the nation – i.e. the psychologically acceptable proportion of national income appropriated through taxation. In Germany, war's impact was rather the reverse. With the support of the USA, a school of economic thought became dominant which argued from the experience of Weimar and fascism that both political and economic stability depended on the vigorous removal of all constraints on free market activity. Cartels were to be broken up, all state bureaucracies removed and taxation was not to be used for demand management. For these theorists, war-time experience simply underlined the negative character of a state-run economy. Industrialists too had grown more wary than ever of state intervention as a result of the war; industrial figures who were too closely associated with Albert Speer, for example, found it hard to gain positions in post-war industry. The result was that the post-1948 economy was less cartelised and concentrated than in Weimar years, with far less state intervention.[18]

In most spheres of social policy, too, the war had only limited impact, often serving merely to underline anxiety about an interventionist state. It had, of course, created a number of new, though temporary, problems for the legislators, above all that of integrating and compensating the expellees. But war did not stimulate or promote innovative solutions or responses to established social problems. In health and pensions policy, in housing and in education, the authorities returned to the established practices of the pre-war era. It is well known that in Britain, victory brought considerable pressure for social reform in the aftermath of both World Wars I and II, but in Germany the idea of making a 'home fit for heroes' hardly applied. The nation was far too concerned to restore the basic features of normal life to attempt major innovations in social policy. In the chaotic conditions of the immediate post-war period, the authorities chose to focus on familiar and established practices. In any case, whatever Germany's politicians and citizens thought in private, it was not possible in the early post-war years to celebrate Germany's soldiers as returning heroes, nor could they harbour any expectations of reward for their military service.[19]

Some innovations from the *pre-war* fascist period survived into the post-war era, particularly when they had themselves built on achievements or developments of Weimar. The promotion of owner-occupied homes in the 1930s, for instance, was considerably extended in the 1950s. The reconstruction of German towns was much facilitated by the extended powers the planners had gained under the Nazis. The 1950s saw a flowering of the type of company social policy so beloved of the DAF. But on the whole, neither fascism nor war left many positive institutional or political legacies in the post-war period.

On the other hand, there is no doubt that the general attitudes towards both democracy and labour on the part of Germany's administrative and managerial elites had been profoundedly affected by the experience of fascism. One of the most reactionary elements of Germany's elite, the *Junker*, had been completely eliminated from the political scene by Nazi purges and the Soviet Occupation. And for the rest, the excesses of the fascist state and the proximity of the Soviet threat combined to create a new awareness of the attractiveness of the Western democratic model, of the need to avoid extremes, of the virtues of a representative political system and the desirability of institutionalised collective bargaining. In other words, what was new was not the institutions – they had been largely created in Weimar – but the commitment to these institutions of those whose job it was to run them and work within them.

IV

What was impact of war on the wider German population and on the working class in particular? We should start by looking at the effects of the Nazis' attempts to control, mobilise and reshape German society during the 1930s.

The first point must be that by 1939 Germany had become a repressive society, full of fear and suspicion. The majority of the population were not overtly subject to direct terror. But everyone knew certain things were best left unsaid, actions best left undone. Through analysis of dreams, through the exaggerated fervour with which Germany's middle classes threw themselves into their private amusements, we can detect the undercurrent of fear that ran through German society. Workers in particular had to be careful, former activists were sent in hundreds of thousands to concentration camps, the individual workers were isolated and political communication became too dangerous in all but the most close-knit of neighbourhoods.[20]

At the same time it was a society that seemed to be working again.

That feeling of being on the brink of disaster that had haunted much of the 1920s and early 1930s was replaced by a new confidence in the social order. Criminality seemed to be decreasing. After the war, even left-wingers and liberals felt bound to acknowledge that the Nazis had appeared capable and purposeful, harnessing social energies in a productive way. The Nazis drew respect from almost all sections of the population for the skill and finesse with which they organised public spectacles and for their success in getting the economy to work.[21]

It was also a society in which class relationships were visibly changing. Though changes in class composition were far from dramatic, there is evidence that mobility from manual to white collar positions increased considerably in the 1930s.[22] Furthermore, quite a number of workers, particularly youngsters in the Hitler Youth, experienced a sort of informal upward mobility outside work by taking on positions of responsibility in Nazi organisations. The status hierarchy had been made more complicated: party ranking offered an alternative status calibration. In addition, the Hitler Youth, sports groups and other organisations were, to a certain extent, able to bring the classes together. Everywhere there was the characteristic and peculiar mixture of Führer-Prinzip and egalitarianism. There are indications that Nazi policy, in conjunction with the spread of mass culture through radio and the cinema, was beginning to change the younger workers' social and self-perceptions. For instance, young miners in the Ruhr abandoned the traditional Sunday dress of an open-necked shirt and cap and opted for the collar and tie. In a small way, they were manifesting the weakening of a working-class subculture and a desire to be citizens in the wider community.[23]

Yet the Nazis were clearly far from winning the loyalty and obedience for which they had hoped. The accelerated re-armaments programme, though it initially benefited from the way the Nazis had disciplined and terrorised the labour movement, actually began to undermine the Nazis' control and integration strategy. The increasing demands placed on the labour force and the awareness of their own power in the tight labour-market led to growing criticism of the regime and a new aggressiveness in wage and other demands. Absenteeism increased and productivity suffered while wages in key economic sectors drifted upwards. By 1939, there were signs that the Nazi labour strategy was crumbling into a familiar pattern of (albeit informal) wage bargaining and material gratification.[24]

These trends and patterns were initially little affected by the outbreak of war. For substantial sections of the population, particularly those not subjected to military call-up, it took a long time for war to make significant changes in their way of life. New features of war-time, such as rationing, had little impact on the general standard of living; real wages held up until 1944. In 1943 there was official opposition to the idea of introducing an evacuation programme for women and children because, it was argued, this would be to disrupt a private sphere hitherto little affected by the war.

For many of those on the home front, it is only in 1942 and 1943 that the war begins to bite, partly because of intensified mobilisation, but even more because the destructive and disruptive capacity of war began to reach home. German casualties rose steeply in the course of the Russian campaign after two years of relatively bloodless combat. In the beginning of 1942, consumers were shocked by a sudden fall in rations. True, they then revived somewhat and stabilised until the closing months of 1944. But other articles began to run short and everyday life became increasingly dominated by shortages. In the winter of 1942–3, for example, areas outside the coal-producing districts received less than a third of their coal requirement. It was above all the increasingly frequent and intensive air raids that disrupted every aspect of normal life. In 1943 there were three times as many bombs as in 1942, and in 1944 five times as many as in 1943. Travel became difficult and time-consuming after bombs disrupted public transport. Many families became homeless. For all this, there was as in Britain, a determination to go on living as normal a life as possible and it was only in the closing months of 1944 that the normal fabric of social life began to disintegrate.[25]

One important effect of the war was to maintain and indeed increase the comparatively high level of geographical and social mobility of the 1930s. On the home front, while most labour directions did not involve moving home, a considerable number of workers found themselves drafted to new areas. Many women and children in the big cities were evacuated to rural communities. For enlisted men, of course, there was a great deal of travel involved. Many accounts of the first years of the war sound – until they reach the Eastern Front – very much like recollections from an extended holiday, a welter of vivid scenes and impressions from strange and colourful countries; the parallel with tourism extends even to the cheap bargains that were to be had at the exchange rates imposed by the Nazis.[26] To paraphrase Clausewitz: war as the continuation of tourism by other means. Much of this mobility was of a temporary nature, yet it seems to have had some long-term significance for those groups which had previously been rather self-enclosed and isolated – the rural communities and also substantial sections of the working class. The war extended the way in which the Nazis in peace-time had already begun – through the media, tourism and mobilisation – to break through the barriers of local consciousness.

At the same time economic mobilisation during the war created new job opportunities and the chance of upward mobility. Retraining programmes, for example, enabled a considerable number of un- or semi-skilled workers to obtain a new qualification and better rates of pay. The army itself offered considerable opportunities for advancement. Such advances were not always easily transferrable to the civil sphere but in practice a good war career proved advantageous at most levels of the post-war job market. For the many workers who became non-comissioned officers and the few who went further, holding positions of authority and responsibility was often a new and important experience which was to inform post-war behaviour.[27]

The influx of foreign forced labour created a form of collective upward mobility for German workers. Since foreigners made up one-quarter of the workforce by the end of the war, many German employees now found themselves elevated to the position of overseers and foremen. In some cases, solidarity developed, particularly where German workers were training their own replacements, as it were, before being sent off to the front. In such cases, the unwilling draftees had an interest in making the training proceed as slowly as possible and needed the foreign trainees help in doing so. But in general, the Nazis were successful in actively involving an increasing number of German workers in the control and repression of the forced labour. From interviews we know that many workers did perceive their new responsibility as a sort of promotion and, just as for their counterparts in the army, the experience of authority was often a significant and lasting one. These experiences of formal and informal social mobility reinforced those of the pre-war period.[28]

At the same time total war meant the intensification of repression and terror and strengthened the tendency to withdraw into the private sphere and to remain guarded and non-committal in public. The individual was isolated and social groups became fragmented.

Another consequence of the war was that labour's attitude to work and the firm begins to shift. Whereas in the late 1930s discontent manifested itself in climbing rates of absenteeism, the war years saw astonishingly stable levels of productivity and absenteeism despite increasingly unfavourable conditions. The more disordered everyday life became, the more attractive was the dependable regularity of the work itself. Even for the conscript labour, the workplace became increasingly a sort of haven and from 1943, the productivity of Russian labour actually rose, amidst deteriorating conditions. For a number of reasons, the interests of labour and employers moved closer together. Both had an interest in protecting plant from call-up and from labour transfers. German labour was given a new role as overseers of the foreign conscripts. And as the employers saw defeat approaching, many were at pains to mend bridges with the labour force.[29]

In general we can say that the war undermined the Nazis' own appeal while reinforcing many of the social changes which they had initiated in the 1930s. It was the increasingly obvious hopelessness of the war that cost the Nazis the last remnants of what limited support they had enjoyed amongst German labour. Yet through isolation and terror, through collective and individual mobility and through the forging of new loyalties and solidarities the war confirmed the Nazis assault on class traditions.

As the conflict approached its conclusion, all these changes paled increasingly in relation to the fight to survive. From the Autumn of 1944 gas and electricity supplies were often missing for large stretches of time in the major cities. In the following spring rations fell below starvation levels. Sybil Bannister wrote in her book, *I lived under Hitler*, that 'Within a few months, with the Allies advancing on all sides, town-dwellers were reduced from a finely organised community to primitive cave-dwellers.' And for the troops, the initially comfortable war on the Western Front and in Africa had been replaced on all sides by an increasingly hopeless and bitter struggle.

In August 1944 the Red Army entered German territory for the first time and from December onwards the mass exodus of refugees from the East began. By the end of the war two-fifths of the German population were on the move – soldiers, evacuees, refugees 'displaced persons' (d.p.'s), former Nazis and so on. Thus the major consequence of the war in the immediate post-war period was the hardship and dislocation that resulted from the destruction of the cities, from economic collapse and from the massive population mobility. The destruction itself was unbelievable. Over 50 per cent of housing in the big cities had been destroyed. Production fell to almost zero in April 1945. In 1946, production in the Western Zones still had not exceeded 25 per cent of pre-war figures. Rations remained little above starvation levels until 1948. For three years after the end of the war, life was one long struggle for the normal citizen.[30]

Though they dominated the immediate post-war period, the hardship and the disruption of normal life were shortlived. Malnutrition disappeared rapidly after 1948. By the mid-1950s unemployment was waning rapidly and living standards exceeded pre-war peaks by a comfortable margin. Enormous strides were made in the housing market. The speed of economic recovery was such as to restore a normal way of life within a few years.

The pace of recovery revealed that, destructive as the war had been, it had left the country's industrial capacity relatively undamaged. Despite bomb-damage and post-war dismantling, the value of industrial plant in 1948 was higher than in 1936. The supply of labour had been harder hit – no less than 25 per cent of the male population in the age range 35–50 had been killed by the war – yet here total war had created its own solution – the refugees and expellees from the east. By 1948 there were getting on for 20 per cent more people available for work in the Western Zones than there had been in 1936.[31]

On the back of economic recovery, the massive number of expellees – by 1950 there were 10 000 000 of them in West Germany – were integrated rapidly. Initially they faced severe problems of adaptation and were particularly hard hit by the high unemployment that followed the currency reform. Yet the tensions between the newcomers and the established community were for the most part temporary and the expellees were quick to find employment. Their party, the BHE, reached its highpoint in the 1953 election with less than 6 per cent of the vote and soon dwindled to insignificance.[32] In other words the destructive and disruptive impact of total war did not present post-war German society with problems it could not solve. Of greater long-term significance for the German working class were the subtler changes to perceptions, behaviour and relationships, above all the weakening of traditional class identities and antipathies which had been wrought by fascism and war.

Yet this is to look into the future. In the immediate post-war period there was good reason to believe that the working class would conform to the Weimar mould. The effect of the capitulation had been to create a power vacuum within Germany and the surviving leaders of the working class movement were keen to realise that synthesis of parliamentary and economic democracy which had already been outlined by labour theoreticians in the Weimar era. The experience of fascism merely underlined the urgency of introducing such a system. True, the fascist experience also convinced the different political groupings within the trade unions of the need to form a united organisation, an innovation which was to be realised in the following years. But otherwise the stage seemed set for a repeat of the political struggles of the post World War I era. However the Allies saw to it that the goal of economic democracy was largely stifled. Labour was prevented from exploiting the collapse of authority within Germany. Just as important was the fact it was not the German employers who prevented it from doing so. It was American power, American intentions and the clear dependence on US aid that made most labour leaders accept fairly rapidly that a capitalist restoration was inevitable. Here and elsewhere the effect of the Allies was to prevent the bitter conflicts between labour and capital that had resulted after 1918 and would otherwise probably have resulted after 1945.[33]

Once the Allies had restrained the reforming impulses of the immediate post-war period and helped to undermine the radical element in the working-class movement, it was Germany's labour leaders themselves who (often unwittingly) ensured that the depoliticisation of everyday life and the diminution of working-class identity achieved by the National Socialists was sustained and strengthened. Nervous of the Communists, uneasy about recreating a divided society and sensitive to the criticism that as a mass organisation they were liable to extremism, labour leaders were at pains to avoid rebuilding a conflict-orientated labour movement. The old workers' cultural organisations were not rebuilt, a concerted effort was made to keep politics out of industrial relations and a co-operative, conciliatory approach towards the employers was adopted. The Social Democrats moved towards the centre and tried to win a middle-class following.

Under these conditions, the integrative, depoliticising tendencies of the Nazi era were able to survive into the post-war period. What emerged, as we know from many surveys in the 1950s, was a hard-working, consumer-orientated, sceptical and unpolitical working class. A strong suspicion of the bosses coexisted with the feeling that labour's status had collectively improved. The boom economy of the 1930s with its possibilities for individual advancement and the toughening experiences of soldiering and surviving the hardships of the Occupation years had encouraged in many workers a confidence in their ability to stand up to those in authority and to profit from the capitalist system. Such individual experiences and the chaos of the pre-1948 rationing system fostered a resigned acceptance of the capitalist system and a recognition of the need for continual rationalisation and modernisation of production. The language of class conflict lost much of its appeal and younger workers in particular did not even understand terms such as 'proletariat'. In their dress, leisure habits and taste younger workers differed little from their bourgeois counterparts. Despite large inequalities in wealth, German society was probably more culturally homogeneous than at any time before or since. In short, even before the economic miracle had had its effect, fascism, war and Allied policy had together created in the working class a far more solid social and ideological base for a democratic capitalist system than had existed in Weimar.[34]

V

It is evident that 'total war' is not an independent cause of social change. Its influence on German society was shaped decisively by the nature of the regime which waged it and that of the regime which followed it. It is true that certain features of the war would have impinged on society no matter what regime was in the power. Any political system would have faced the need to mobilise all possible reserves of labour, materials and energy for the war effort. No regime could wish away the destructive capability of the enemy's weapons. But the way the Nazis responded to such challenges and opportunities and the way the Allies' post-war policies refracted and channelled the experiences and wishes that were the legacy of war were as important in shaping its impact as any such 'objective' features of war itself. This would be a point of lesser interest in a country where, as in Britain, the only changes in the political system were those brought about by the needs of war. But in Germany, the political discontinuities make it of crucial importance.

Partly because of these discontinuities, total war does not stand out as a revolutionary impulse in the way that it perhaps does in some other countries. Even where it stimulated or impelled the Nazis to introduce quite new policies, it is often the specifically National Socialist flavour of these measures that is striking and that carried the greatest potential for social change. In any case, war was slow to bring any changes at all. Many of the innovations necessary for a nationally co-ordinated and concerted war effort had been carried out already, in some cases in advance calculation of war-time requirements, in others because mobilising society's energies for the national cause was a central goal of the National Socialists.

Nevertheless, the war did have a specific impact which differed from the preceding period. In the first place, it intensified the Nazi assault on established milieus, the fragmentation of social groups and the isolation of the individual. Secondly, for the German workers, the experience of destruction and dislocation and of common interests with the employers – vis à vis the Nazi state and later the Occupying Powers – prepared the way for the pragmatic acceptance of the capitalist system. Thus war was preparing the ground for Western Germany's return to capitalist democracy even before total defeat brought the fall of the Nazi regime.

Notes

1. Footnotes are intended to provide an indicative bibliography only and no attempt at comprehensive or systematic references has been made. For general accounts of social change in this period see David Schoenbaum, *Hitler's Social Revolution: Class and Status in Nazi Germany* (New York, 1966); Detlev Peukert, *Volksgenossen und Gemeinschaftsfremde: Anpassung, Ausmerze und Aufbegehren unter dem Nationalsozialismus* (Cologne, 1982); Werner Conze und M. Rainer Lepsius (eds) *Sozialgeschichte der BRD* (Stuttgart, 1983); R. Dahrendorf, *Society and democracy in Germany* (London, 1968).
2. On wartime social policy see Marie-Luise Recker, *Nationalsozialistische Sozialpolitik im 2.Weltkrieg* München, 1985). For labour policy specifically, see Wolfgang Werner, *Bleib übrig: Deutsche Arbeiter in der nationalsozialistischen Kriegswirtschaft* (Düsseldorf, 1983).
3. The most comprehensive account of German mobilisation is Ludolf Herbst, *Der Totale Krieg und die Ordnung der Wirtschaft: Die Kriegswirtschaft im Spannungsfeld von Politik, Ideologie und Propaganda 1939–1945* (Stuttgart, 1982).
4. See Volker Berghahn, *The Americanisation of German Industry* (Leamington Spa, 1986), introduction.
5. For a view which places more emphasis on changes in the 1939–41 period, see Richard J. Overy, 'Hitler's War and the German Economy. A reinterpretation', *Economic History Review* (1982) XXXV, 2, pp. 277–91.
6. See Recker, *NS Sozialpolitik* and Werner, *Bleib übrig.*
7. Timothy W. Mason, *Sozialpolitik im Dritten Reich: Arbeiterklasse und Volksgemeinschaft* (Opladen, 1977) passim.
8. Werner, *Bleib übrig*, pp. 220ff.
9. On the competition between the DAF and other elements of the Nazi regime, see for example, Gunther Mai, ' "Warum steht der deutsche Arbeiter zu Hitler?" Zur Rolle der Deutschen Arbeitsfront im Herrschaftssystem des Dritten Reiches', in *Geschichte und Gesellschaft* (1986) 12,2,212,–34.

10. On women in Nazi Germany see Jill Stephenson, *Women in Nazi Society* (London, 1975) and Dörte Winkler, *Frauenarbeit im "Dritten Reich"* (Hamburg, 1977).
11. On social political initiatives towards labour see Schoenbaum, *Hitler's Social Revolution* and the essays by Reulecke and others in Detlev Peukert and Jürgen Reulecke (eds), *Die Reihen fast geschlossen. Beiträge zur Geschichte des Alltags unterm Nationalsozialismus* (Wuppertal, 1981). See also Günther Mai, 'Warum steht der deutscher Arbeiter zu Hitler'.
12. Werner, *Bleib übrig*, esp pp. 277ff.
13. Richard Grunberger, *A Social History of the Third Reich* (Harmondsworth, 1971) contains a useful description of the impact of Nazi terror. A systematic account can be found in Hans Buchheim *et al.* (eds) *Anatomie des SS-Staates*, 2 vols (Munich, 1967).
14. See Berghahn, *Americanisation*, introduction; Hans Mommsen, 'Die Realisierung des Utopischen: Die Endlösung der Judenfrage im "Dritten Reich" ', in *Geschichte und Gesellschaft* (1983) 9, 381–420.
15. Grunberger, *A Social History*, p. 63.
16. The standard work on forced labour is now Ulrich Herbert, *Fremdarbeiter: Politik und Praxis des "Ausländer-Einsatzes" in der Kriegswirtschaft des Dritten Reiches* (Berlin, Bonn, 1985).
17. For a good general discussion of the balance between restorative and innovative elements in the post-war settlement see Jürgen Kocka, '1945: Neubeginn oder Restauration', in Carola Stern und Heinrich August Winkler (eds) *Wendepunkte deutscher Geschichte 1848–1945* (Frankfurt, 1979) pp. 141–68.
18. See here Berghahn, *Americanisation*, passim.
19. See for instance Hans Günther Hockerts, *Sozialpolitische Entscheidungen im Nachkriegsdeutschland 1945–1947* (Stuttgart, 1980).
20. Detlev Peukert, *Volksgenossen und Gemeinschaftsfremde*, passim.
21. See Ian Kershaw, *Der Hitler-Mythos: Volksmeinung und Propaganda im Dritten Reich* (Stuttgart, 1980).
22. See the discussion of mobility in Josef Mooser, *Arbeiterleben in Deutschland 1900–1970* (Frankfurt/M, 1984) pp. 113ff.
23. On class and status see Schoenbaum, *Hitlers Social Revolution*. Michael Zimmermann, 'Ausbruchshoffnungen: Junge Bergleute in den Dreißiger Jahren', in Lutz Niethammer (ed) *"Die Jahre weiß man nicht, wo man die heute hinsetzen soll". Faschismuserfahrungen im Ruhrgebiet* (Berlin, Bonn, 1983) pp. 97–132.
24. These trends are well documented in Mason, *Sozialpolitik*.
25. See Werner, *Bleib übrig* and Lutz Niethammer, 'Heimat und Front. Versuch, zehn Kriegerinnerungen aus der Arbeiterklasse des Ruhrgebietes zu verstehen', in Niethmammer (ed) *Die Jahre weiß man nicht*, pp. 163–232.
26. See Niethammer, 'Heimat und Front'.
27. There is no satisfactory account of the impact of war-time experience on post-war labour. See Niethammer, 'Heimat und Front' and my PhD thesis, 'New Labour in the Ruhr Mines' (Warwick University, 1987).
28. In addition to Ulrich Herbert's study referred to above, see also his

essay 'Apartheid nebenan. Erinnerungen an die Fremdarbeiter im Ruhrgebiet', in Niethammer (ed.), *Die Jahre weiß man nicht,* pp. 233–66.

29. Both Herbert and Werner draw attention to the factory's role as a refuge. One employers' changing attitudes, see Günther Mai, 'Warum steht der deutsche Arbeiter zu Hitler', esp. p. 232. See also John Gillingham, *Industry and Politics in the Third Reich* (Methuen, 1985).

30. For an introduction to conditions after the war, see Manfred Overesch, *Deutschland 1945–1949: Vorgeschichte und Gründung der Bundesrepublik* (Königsten/Ts, 1979).

31. The standard work on the recovery is Werner Abelshauser, *Wirtschaft in Westdeutschland 1945–1948: Rekonstruktion und Wiederaufbaubedingungen in der amerikanischen und britischen Zonen,* Stuttgart, 1975).

32. For a good survey of recent work on the refugees see Wolfgang Benz (ed) *Die Vertreibung der Deutschen aus dem Osten: Ursachen, Ereignisse, Folgen* (Frankfurt/M, 1985).

33. An excellent introduction to the post-war labour movement is to be found in Lutz Niethammer, 'Rekonstruktion und Desintegration: Zum Verständnis der deutschen Arbeiterbewegung zwischen Krieg und kaltem· Krieg', in Winkler (ed.), *Politische Weichenstellungen in Nchkriegsdeutschland 1945–1953* (Göttingen, 1979) pp. 26–43.

34. Among many other studies see H. Popitz and P. Bahrdt, *Das Gesellschaftbild des Arbeiters* (Tübingen, 1961); H. Schelsky, *Die skeptische Generation* (Düsseldorf, 1963); Helmuth Croon und K. Utermann, *Zeche und Gemeinde: Untersuchungen über den Strukturwandel einer Zechengemeinde im nördlichen Ruhrgebiet* (Tübingen, 1958); Frank Deppe, *Das Bewußtsein der Arbeiter: Studien zur politischen Soziologie des Arbeiterbewußtseins* (Köln, 1971). In English, see Angi Rutter, 'Elites, Estate and Strata: Class in West Germany since 1945; in Arthur Marwick (ed.) *Class in the Twentieth Century* (Brighton and New York, 1986), pp. 115–64.

6 World War II and Social Change in France

François Bédarida

Trying to evaluate the impact of World War II on French society is a far from easy task. Not only because the components of the problem are multiple and complex, but still more because of the methodological difficulties involved. To what extent, for example, can one speak of continuity between the war and the post-war period? Because of its seminal influence on post-war developments, could the war be called a matrix or crucible? But would that not be to reason by hindsight? On the other hand, how does one measure the roles, respectively, of long-term factors and short-term factors, of secular trends and immediate events? Did the war act as an accelerator or a brake upon existing processes of change? How can one distinguish between what was a consequence of the world conflict and what simply happened at the same time?

There is a further difficulty: the specificity of the French case compared with that of the other belligerents. Here one can cite three striking facts. The first, the profound commotion created in the collective memory by the years 1939 to 1945. These 'black years', these 'sombre years', as they are called, continue right up to our own day to be scorching years, so traumatic was the experience lived through by the French: the drama of a society, a nation, a state all put in danger of their very existence. In this respect it truly was a *total* war, whose ramifications were at once military, national, political, social, psychological and moral.

Hence the intensity of the passions and the violence of the controversies evoked. Eloquent witness is born by the *affaires* in the recent past, which, relayed by the media, shook the collective conscience: the *affaire* Barbie of 1983–7, that is to say from the arrest to the trial; the *affaire* Manouchian in 1985 (in connection with a television film tracing the activities of communist Jewish groups in Paris in 1942–3); the *affaire* Roques in 1986 (stirred up by a university thesis leaning towards a denial of the existence of the gas chambers);

the *affaire* Marenches in 1986–7 (following statements by a retired chief of the secret services claiming that celebrated resistance fighters were in fact Gestapo agents). Does not all this prove that the drama of 1939 to 1945 is still running?

A second aspect of the specificity of the French case is the paradoxical character of the effects of the war on France. In contrast with World War I which, despite resulting in glorious victory, hit France in its very vitals, World War II created a new dynamic. Above all because it expressed itself through an astonishing reversal of fortune and destiny, since France experienced in turn defeat and victory: complete collapse (collapse of the army, the government, the State, the nation), invasion and occupation on the one hand; liberation, recovery and victory on the other. So France was both loser and winner.

Another paradoxical feature is that, from a long-term historical perspective, the war has been the point of departure of a period of unprecedented growth. Demographic growth (the French population, stuck at around 40 000 000 for half a century, rose in the space of forty years to 55 000 000, an increase of 40 per cent) and economic growth – the war ushered in what has been called '*les trente glorieuses*' (1945–75). Today the contrast is staggering, as it is in Germany and Italy, between the misery and destruction left by the war and the prosperity and well-being resulting from growth and modernisation.

The third striking fact is that the years 1939–45 are located at the centre of two great historiographical debates over the development of French society in the twentieth century. On one side is the debate over archaism and modernity. According to the traditional account, put forward by figures such as Alfred Sauvy or Jean Fourastié, and which for thirty years has been widely accepted, France passed in the aftermath of the war, thanks to modernisation and state planning, from economic and demographic stagnation ('*le malthusianisme français*') to growth. In the light of the experience of recession and defeat, the old suffocating restrictions were blasted out of existence, and old attitudes overturned. Here was the start of a new era, after decades of economic deceleration and demographic exhaustion and after the '*Sedan économique*' of the crisis of the 1930s and the Occupation. Against this account – articulated, it is worth noting, by the 'modernisers' themselves – there has been developing for several years a 'revisionist' school, represented by such historians as Jean Bouvier, Maurice Lévy-Leboyer and Patrick Fridenson, according to whom the growth and dynamism of the French economy since the industrialisation of the nineteenth century has been grossly underestimated, and who place seriously in doubt the contrast between flagging pre-war years and dazzling post-war ones.[1]

Another historiographical debate has been raging for several years. This concerns the nature of the Vichy regime and its place in the 'continuum' of French history. Should one see in the period 1940–4 a caesura or a parenthesis in the evolution of France, or are there continuities prevailing in the field of civil society, social movements and collective mentalities? According to the traditional account – an account which is ideological as much as historical – between the pre-war period and the post-war period there was a rapid and chaotic succession of three distinctively different phases: the expiring Third Republic, the Vichy regime (in continuous decline from 1940 to 1944), the liberation and the Fourth Republic. But, little by little, this rigid conceptualisation has been replaced by a more sophisticated, less epochal, view bringing out the lines of continuity between the regimes and placing the period 1940 to 1944 in the longer-term perspective of the evolution of French society, involving the crisis of society and State, the constraints upon modernisation, the search for appropriate and efficient institutions, and the aspiration for a social *new deal*. In the footsteps of Stanley Hoffmann, French historians in growing numbers have explored these new paths full of illuminating re-interpretations.[2]

THE ORDEAL OF WAR

Faced with the test of total war, France went through a crisis which was more the crisis of a nation than the crisis of a society. My contention is that during the war years the structural, quantitative and institutional changes were much less important than was the qualitative or psychological impact. But these changes in mentalities and collective culture under the shock of the war generated in the aftermath a dynamic transformation, which can be expressed in terms of structure, quantitative development and institutional processes. In other words World War II affected the soul still more than the body of France, liberating new energies for new ventures.

In the demographic sphere, in spite of the grief and the suffering, the results turned out contrary to the most sombre expectations and the pessimistic prognostications were totally contradicted by the facts. Not only did civil mortality increase by no more than 5 per cent in comparison with the pre-war rate (and infantile mortality scarcely more), with constant figures across the social classes, but the principal surprise arose in connection with the birth rate which rose sharply from 1942 onwards. In contrast with the pre-war years the continued propagation of the nation began to seem assured. One can speak of a U-turn of fertility. The contrast with World War I is startling: thus Sauvy has calculated that from 1915 to 1919 there were 2 246 000 births, while from 1940 to 1944 the total of births reached 2 754 000, which represents 500 000 young people more.[3] By the same token, if one compares households formed in 1925 and in 1943, the former on average comprised 1.98 children per couple, the latter 2.35. As for the hecatomb of war losses, it had been far heavier in 1914–18 than in 1939–45. It is a symbolic fact that while in 1934 the total of pensions dispensed to widows, orphans and war-wounded reached 2 500 000, in 1950 it was only 214 000.[4]

As for the economy, it suffered greatly. Here the balance sheet is dramatic, much more serious than in 1918, by virtue of both the greater material destruction and the economic pillage of the occupying power. Thus 74 *départements* were affected by the war, compared with 13 between 1914 and 1918. Nearly a quarter of domestic housing, some of it however already run down, was destroyed. Out of 40 000 km of railway track, no more than 18 000 km remained in service. And the situation was worse for rolling stock; only 1 out of 6 locomotives was in working order, 1 goods wagon in 3, and 1 passenger carriage in 2.

As to the magnitude of the French contribution to the German economy, it reached an appalling level. According to Alan Milward's calculations, out of the occupation levies paid by France, Holland, Belgium, Norway, Bohemia and Poland, the French contribution can be estimated at 42 per cent of the total. In every year of the occupation the total of payments was greater than the whole French revenue from taxation. As a percentage of French national income in 1938 at 1938 prices, the payments to Germany from France amounted to one-tenth in 1940, one-fifth in 1942, and more than one-third in 1943.[5] The most visible phenomenon, and that which most forcibly struck public opinion, was the low level of nutrition. Undernourishment and malnutrition affected all categories of the population, but most particularly the town dwellers, while the black market aggravated social inequalities. On average the food ration amounted to 1200 calories per adult per day, something less than half of the pre-war consumption. Here there is scope for a series of studies of the impact of this malnutrition on French society (it lasted until 1948–9), for this fine territory for historical investigation remains practically virgin.[6] But these circumstances scarcely modified the basic structures of French society. Studies conducted on the active population and on business enterprises and the workforce show little change in the distribution of social classes and employment. What prevailed, on the contrary, was a manifest stability, and by every calculation the fluctuations were weak. From the census of 1936 to that of 1946, the division by main sector of activity remained practically identical, as the following table shows[7]:

Table 6.1   Main sectors of economic activity

	Primary(%)	Secondary (%)	Tertiary (%)
1921	43	29	28
1936	37.4	29.9	32.7
1946	37.2	30.5	32.2

What emerges is that, by comparison with the secular trend, the war slowed down the decline in the numbers employed in the traditional sectors (agriculture, mines, clothing), and that in the modern sectors (metallurgy, chemicals, building) it had retarded the development which otherwise would have taken place. But in a series of economic activities, involving industry, commerce and the service trades, the war's influence was nil. In sum, as far as the active population are concerned, its effects prolonged those of the 1930s.

It is the same story with business enterprises. A recent colloquium at the Institut d'Histoire du Temps Présent on the evolution of business enterprise during World War II based on departmental and local studies showed that in the short term continuity predominates.[8] Pre-war tendencies prevail with respect to the entire industrial fabric (structure, size, ownership, geographical location) and the methods and types of production. The war had little influence on industrial concentration, on the shape of business enterprise, or on the distribution of wage-earners. And all of that in an economy of scarcity: scarcity of primary materials, scarcity of machines, scarcity of spare parts, scarcity of transport, scarcity of manpower (taking account of prisoners of war and workers transported to Germany).

On the other hand, one must be aware of certain modifications in economic and social geography (for example at Lyons and in the Lyonnaise region, where chemicals had become the premier industry in 1946, whereas textiles had held the lead until 1936) as well as in technological processes where progress was accelerated by the war (use of plastics in the chemicals industry and special steels in metallurgy).

From the point of view of relations between the classes, the war endorsed and accentuated the existing state of affairs, save with respect to one area, the relationship between town and country. As a result of the widespread shortages the peasants, the producers and purveyors of foodstuffs, acquired the dominant and privileged position, and they benefited greatly from inflation and the black market. Here we do have a reversal of a pre-war trend, but a temporary reversal, directly related to immediate circumstances, and one which disappeared towards the end of the 1940s when the food supply situation returned to normal. Apart from this temporary phenomenon, social mobility changed little, while class divisions tended to sharpen.

It is in fact in the sphere of mentalities, in the spirit of the country, that the disruption of the war is most marked in its effects on French society. A society traumatised by defeat struggled with everyday life, uncertain of its own future. The violence of the shock shook belief, symbols and values. It was a crisis of the entire nation, a crisis which would leave enduring traces. Wherever one looks throughout the national territory or its inhabitants, the country was dislocated, torn, in tatters. Anyway where was the national territory? In the occupied zone, in the 'free zone', in the 'prohibited' zone, in the Nord-Pas-de-Calais attached to the military administration of Belgium, in Alsace-Lorraine annexed by Germany, in London with the Free French, in the empire which slowly rallied to De Gaulle? One does not know. On the other hand, with all the population movements, the exodus of 1940, the refugees, the prisoners of war, compulsory labour service, deportation, there was an extraordinary mixing up of the population. On all sides, loyalties inter-twined and were at war with each other. *Vichyssois, pétainistes, résistants, 'attentistes'* (those, the majority, who awaited the end of the war without declaring for one side or the other), collaborators, Free French, prisoners of war in Germany (two million in 1940, still more than a million in 1944/45), *Alsaciens-Lorrains* forced into military service: the diversity of experience together with the outrages suffered explain very well the lines of fracture which survive into our own time.

With good cause the economist F. L. Closon entitled his memoirs of Free France and the Resistance *Le temps des passions*. These simmering passions are, for example, demonstrated by the dramatic dialogue between Captain Henri Frenay, one of the chief leaders of the

Resistance, and his mother, herself the wife of an officer. 'You are going to do harm to our country,' his mother said to him, 'and you will do it thoroughly as you do everything. And you think that I shall keep quiet, let you do it! . . . I love you tenderly, as you know, for my children are my whole life . . ., but above maternal love is love of country. I shall denounce you to the police in order to prevent you from doing harm . . .' And Frenay replied to his mother: 'I respect your conscience, you must respect what commands mine. But if you carry out your threat, do not summon me to your death bed for I shall not come'. And he adds: 'I kissed her. We parted, we did not see each other again till the Liberation. I was a member of the government. She had not denounced me.'[9]

In this climate of exacerbated passions it is not surprising that the year 1944 holds a special place in what has been called 'the Franco-French wars'. Old hatreds were joined to new fissures in this period of 'sorrow and pity' to the extent that intestine struggles threatened dangerously to split national unity, all of this against the background of world conflict.[10] A war of ideologies (not a war of classes), a severe destabilisation of the State and of society, fratricidal combats between French nationals (police and *Milice* on one side, the *maquis* on the other): these were the three factors which crashed against each other and brought France to the edge of civil war. But however violent these circumstances, one must, in order to assess their exact significance, compare them with other experiences in both time and space, thus making it possible to evaluate them and set them in context. In comparison with the bloodshed in the past history of France, at the time of the Commune, the June days of 1848, or the *Vendée*, the balance sheet appears distinctively less heavy. And by comparison with the tragic events unfolding at the same moment in other parts of Europe, the ravages of the Franco-French war of 1940–4 are far from being comparable with the civil wars which ravaged Greece or Yugoslavia.

Certainly people have expatiated greatly – and exaggerated greatly – on the *épuration* which followed the Liberation. An explosive dossier, where one finds pell-mell all the traumas of the black years, anguish and grief, hatred and rancour, disillusionment at the time and distortion subsequently of the collective memory. But the territory today has been amply worked over by historians, thus enabling us to pronounce judicially on the legend of the 'blood bath'. A thoroughly painstaking investigation, instituted twenty years ago by the Comité d'Histoire de la Deuxième Guerre Mondiale, and continued by the

Institut d'Histoire du Temps Présent, *département* by *département*, canton by canton, shows that the figure for summary executions – the central controversial issue – is lower than 9000. So far we have the statistics of 76 *départements* out of 87 (if one excludes the three *départements* of Alsace-Lorraine): the total of summary executions stands at 7300, of which 2000 took place before the Normandy landings, 4000 between 6 June and the Liberation, and 1300 after the Liberation.[11] These figures concur with the scholarly estimates formulated by Peter Novick in 1968[12] and, more curiously, with the total given by General De Gaulle as early as 1959 in his *Mémoires de Guerre*, that is to say 10 842 summary executions.[13] To these must be added the figure for legal executions, that is to say those carried out after judgement by the tribunals. The total is of 1393 judicial executions (it must be remembered that two-thirds of those condemned to death were reprieved by the head of the provisional government). In other words the balance sheet for repression at the Liberation stands at around 10 000 deaths – a figure which has nothing in common with the widely circulated myths.

With respect to the legal *épuration*, if the figure for individuals arrested, interned and prosecuted in 1944–5 amounts to 125 000, the percentage is distinctly lower than in the other countries of western Europe: 1 per thousand in France against 4 per thousand in the Netherlands and 6 per thousand in Belgium and in Norway (for its part the Vichy government had condemned 135 000 individuals, dismissed 35 000 civil servants and demoted 15 000 officers).[14]

In the same way the geography of the repression does not correspond at all with that transmitted by the collective memory. The highest number of summary executions relative to population took place in such *départements* as the Dordogne, Haute-Savoie, the Côtes-du-Nord, the Aube, the Haute-Saône, while in the *départements* reputed to be 'hot', like the Haute-Garonne, Gard and Var, the levels were quite low. Exit the myth of the Midi red with blood and Bolshevism . . . In the end, in the encounter with contradictory clichés – clichés of the Right designed to inspire belief in a distorted justice across classes, clichés of the Left accusing the *épuration* of having only dealt with 'little men' whilst sparing the 'big ones' – the minute analysis of the departmental statistics reveals that the proportions of those purged by social category corresponds, in broad terms, with the socio-professional composition of the *département*.

Indeed one cannot comprehend the phenomenon of the *épuration* if one does not grasp its fundamental paradox. For De Gaulle and his government, the goal was to use it as an instrument of national reconciliation. Cutting across the contemporary order of the day, 'punish the traitors', it was a question of appealing to the French to join together in a great collective project: the reconstruction of France.[15] However, in the consciousness which the French had of their collective identity, and of the place of their country in the world, doubts persisted. Certainly, in the atmosphere of exaltation of the Liberation, a wave of nationalism won over a large part of public opinion. According to an opinion poll of December 1944, 64 per cent of French people thought that their country had recovered its position as a great power. Another poll in March 1945 put at 67 per cent the number of those who coveted the left bank of the Rhine as in the finest moments of Foch and Clemenceau![16] Had the humiliations of 1940 been effaced? In reality these illusions did not last long; very quickly scepticism – and realism – returned. In a course of public lectures presented in 1947–8 Raymond Aron noted 'a form of indifference to the destiny of France', an indifference nourished by the conviction that the national future was being played for outside the country, decided by forces exterior, or superior, to anything which the French themselves could do.[17]

THE EFFECTS OF WAR: REVOLUTION OR RESTORATION?

Combat, one of the oldest and most glorious of the clandestine newspapers, and which had a fine career in the immediate post-war period, proudly unfurled the motto 'From the Resistance to the revolution'. In effect, at the Liberation, everybody spoke of revolution – apart from De Gaulle who preferred the term 'renovation'. But the fashionable rhetoric had not the slightest practical application in the real world. Very soon one witnessed the restoration of the State, and it was *'l'ordre républicain'* which triumphed, without there being a serious struggle by the Communist party to seize power. In brief, society was neither overthrown by the communist revolution which some people feared nor by the advent of a humanistic socialism of the sort advocated in Resistance circles. Without question, the social changes generated by the war form part of a process of *evolution*, not of *revolution*.

All of which is not to say that they should be under-estimated. But these changes of World War II, which produced effects in the medium term, if not in the long term, are *measured* and *nuanced*. They can be analysed from many different angles. For myself, I shall approach them through four key problems which appear to me of special significance for the understanding of French society: elites, women, religion and the role of the State.

To what extend did the Liberation result in a renewal of the country's elites? At first sight the circumstances seem favourable: had not the elites of the Third Republic been discredited by the defeat of 1940? Had not those of Vichy been swamped in the opprobrium attaching to that fallen regime? Accordingly, everyone was agreed in thinking that liberated France would have to depend upon new elites if it desired reconstruction, democratisation, modernisation and the re-conquest of the world position temporarily lost.

Incontrovertibly there was a shift within the political élites. New men, fresh from the clandestine struggle, now occupied the corridors of power. They were the ones who directed the government and held the ministerial portfolios in place of the figures of the Third Republic (Daladier never recovered from Munich, Reynaud was destroyed by the events of May to June 1940; Herriot was all but a shadow after the war; the only figure of importance rescued from pre-war days was Henri Queuille). In the parliamentary assemblies, the phenomenon was no less marked: deputies and senators from the Third Republic had for the most part been cleared out and largely replaced by men (and some women) from the Resistance. The numerical importance of *Résistants* among those elected to the assemblies was to be one of the characteristics of the Fourth Republic throughout its entire existence, even if many notables in the localities survived all changes of regime.[18]

However, the élites issuing from the clandestine movements, in spite of the legitimacy which the Resistance gave them, found themselves faced by a difficult challenge. In effect, the prestige which attached to those who had been, as was said then, 'heroes of the Resistance' derived from what was widely recognised as their possession of élite characteristics, in the moral sense of the term: they formed an élite of courage, of self-denial and of moral value. It thus seemed normal, after an ordeal of that intensity, to recognise their exceptional prowess in trusting to them high social and political responsibilities. Now, just as soon as this élite was invested with power, the problems which urgently required solution were problems of a totally different order, technical problems, problems of management and organisation. The touchstone henceforth was not bravery, but technical expertise, ability and political competence. From that sprang many defeats and much disillusionment. Nothing necessarily qualified a *maquis* chief, a manager of a clandestine newspaper, or a member of a intelligence network to become overnight a deputy or minister, a director of a nationalised industry, or the holder of a top post in the civil service. On the other hand it is incontestable that the Resistance did constitute a nursery for new talents, and it is no accident that in 1985–6, that is to say forty years after the end of the war, three of the highest posts in the State were occupied by men from the Resistance: the presidency of the Republic (François Mitterrand), the presidency of the National Assembly (Jacques Chaban-Delmas), the presidency of the *Conseil Constitutionnel* (Daniel Mayer).

With regard to the economic élites, at first sight continuity seems to dominate. But one far from negligible filter was in operation: the economic *épuration* – a moderate, but significant, purge – along with the emergence of new centres of decision-making such as the *Commissariat du Plan* and the large nationalised enterprises (Renault, EDF, etc.).[19] Certainly there was no class purge, such as demanded by the CGT, against the 'trusts' and the '*deux cent familles*', but there was, at the level of mentalities, profound regeneration both in business enterprises and in administration. Hence the formation of a modernising elite which took control of the commanding heights of the economy, here through new men taking positions of power, there through amalgamation with directors from former times. It was this change and this coming together in a spirit of competence, efficiency, renovation and social peace which constitutes one of the keys to the great economic growth of the 1950s and 1960s.

By contrast, the place of women in this promotion of new élites could scarcely be more restricted. The changes brought to the condition of women by the second world conflict have been greatly exaggerated, both at the time and during the immediate post-war period. People have been too quick to interpret the Resistance as a demonstration of progress towards equality of the sexes. On the other side we perhaps have a tendency today to under-estimate the changes. Within the workplace changes in employment were qualitatively real, though quantitatively slight. If the female working population increased both absolutely and relatively from 1936 to 1946 (an increase of 560 000 individuals), the figures have to be corrected, because they include agriculture where they were over-estimated. If agriculture is left out, the proportion of women in employment only rises from 20.6 per cent to 22 per cent.[20]

On the other hand, to the extent that the Resistance served as a channel for social promotion, one might well think that women, who played an irreplaceable role, would also benefit from this. But all studies on this theme have illuminated how far in reality they became the 'forgotten people' of history. Besides, even in their clandestine activities, women were for most of the time confined within their traditional roles, above all carrying out subordinate secretarial or social service work. Here for example are the terms in which a leading figure described the work of one of his female collaborators: 'Like all her female comrades, she had the worst job, typing letters, fetching and carrying the mail, putting people in touch with each other, taking part in secret rendezvous, emptying our letter boxes, clandestine and under surveillance, seeking out meeting places, and, whenever that became necessary, doing the shopping with genuine or forged ration books.' And he concludes that if 'the women of the Resistance had their place, their important place in all the networks,' in the end 'they were the Marthas of the clandestine movements.'[21]

One must not minimise to the same extent the progress made, in particular with regard to the acquisition of the vote, a right which suffragist women, in spite of all their efforts, had not been able to gain between 1919 and 1938, in particular because of the opposition of the Senate dominated by the Radicals. Again in 1944, when the Conseil National de la Résistance wanted to include votes for women in its programme, the Radical party tried to obstruct this,[22] but without success, for the text adopted on 15 March 1944 recognised the old feminist claim: to become citizens. At the same time, and on the same subject, De Gaulle in a speech of 18 March 1944 declared: 'to establish democracy renewed in its institutions and above all in its practices, the new regime must be based on representatives elected by all men and all women of our country.' Consequently, the ordinance drawn up in Algiers in April 1944 by the Comité Français de Libération Nationale on the constitutional organisation to be set up at the Liberation specified: 'Women are voters and candidates under the same condition as men.' The new right was exercised for the first time in the municipal elections (29 April), then at the time of the referendum and the legislative elections for the constituent assembly (21 October).

This revolution in basic principles was fully achieved in the Declaration of Rights placed at the head of the Constitution of 1946. While the first article declared, 'All men, and all women are born and live free and equal before the law', the second clause added, as the result of a campaign orchestrated by the Union des Femmes Françaises, a para-Communist organisation. 'The law guarantees to women equal rights to those of men in every domain.' But the familial vocation of women was explicitly recalled by article 24 which tried to reconcile equality of the sexes with specifically feminine characteristics: 'The nation protects all mothers and all children through appropriate legislation and institutions. It guarantees to woman the exercise of her functions as citizen and worker in conditions which permit her to fulfil her role as mother and her social function.' One can see here how potent the traditional mould remained and how slowly the relations between men and women evolved.

Where, by contrast, a considerable transformation took place was in the connection between religion and society. Not only was a new brand of secularism introduced, allowing Catholics to be reintegrated into public life, but Catholicism suddenly pervaded the whole civil society. It is true that French Catholicism was then undergoing a process of renewal, theological, pastoral and liturgical. At the same time it was the war which gave birth to the experience of the worker-priests. It was in the middle of the war that the famous book, *France, pays de mission?*, which sounded the alarm over the depth and extent of the decline in Christianity, was published. It was in face of the great crisis of conscience provoked by the war and by the immediate post-war period – and in spite of the support given to Vichy by most bishops – that the advanced wing of Catholicism affirmed its position (*Témoignage Chrétien, Temps Présent, Esprit, Jeunesse de l'Eglise*, etc.). Whether in the political realm, with the creation and rise of the Mouvement Républicain Populaire, the trade union sphere with the CFTC, the domain of youth and culture with the JOC, the JEC, the JAC, in the media (in particular the press), in economic modernisation, in intellectual life, everywhere could be seen the vitality of a Catholicism which was to pervade everyday life, and the entire social fabric.

Finally, World War II contributed to the growth in the power of the State and to shaping in a new and specific manner the relation between the State and the citizen; the latter in a three-fold manner. First there was a social and economic *new deal*, formed by the triangle, Social Security–Nationalisation–Planning. The aspiration towards a new social order both reformist and progressive, in place of the '*désordre établi*' of the pre-war years and the paternalism of Vichy, thus issued in a Welfare State *à la Française*: an enduring state of affairs and one to which the French today are very attached, as all opinion polls demonstrate (here there is a striking parallel with the evolution of British society).

In the second place modernisation has operated within the framework of *dirigisme* and *étatisme*. The trend here was not new, but as Richard Kuisel has brilliantly shown in his analysis of the relations between capitalism and the State, the years 1930 to 1950 constitute a decisive stage in a long-standing process, initiated with World War I, but which reached its climax during and immediately after World War II.[23] In the course of this transition from a liberal economy, prudent and with limited aspirations, towards a directed, planned and dynamic economy, the battle for modernisation was won, thanks to the decisive intervention of the State. But within the framework of this mixed economy, management and *dirigisme* helped and reinforced each other. Thus a special relationship was created between the State (i.e. the government and the civil servants) on one side and the entrepreneurs on the other.

Here is the third panel of the triptych: from the heritage of Vichy, the aspirations of the Resistance, the conquests of the Liberation, there arose a presence of the State more and more accentuated in the collective life. It has been possible to speak with reference to the Vichy government, of '*rage réglementaire*' ('mania for regulation'). Now, from this point of view, the post-war period, far from marking a discontinuity, followed in the same direction. This resulted in a multiplication of the interventions of the authorities in the ordinary everyday business of life. This taking charge of the social by the State showed itself in every domain, youth, food supply, factory inspection, culture, theatre, sport and, above all, social work.[24] In this regard, the war was indubitably the generator of a considerable transformation.

In conclusion, in spite of the disappointments and the disillusionment of the Liberation and the reconstruction, in spite of the obliteration of the ambitions, the expectations and the hopes of the Resistance,[25] French society after 1945 experienced neither revolution nor restoration. The new social contract, product of the years of war, was based upon two driving forces: social innovation and national tradition. Hence there was no redistribution of power but a new social balance. Thus World War II should be set in the context of a process of crisis, reshaping, and transformation, lasting from the 1930s to the early 1950s, a process to which it gave a decisive impetus.

Notes

1. As a manifesto of the 'revisionist' school, see a recent publication: P. Fridenson and A. Straus (eds) *Le capitalisme français XIX-XXème siècle: blocages et dynamismes d' une croissance* (Paris, 1987). See also F. Bloch-Lainé and J. Bouvier, *La France Restaurée 1944–1954* (Paris, 1985).

2. See Stanley Hoffmann's seminal article, 'The Effects of World War II on French Society and Politics', *French Historical Studies*, vol. ii, 1, (Spring, 1961), pp. 28–63. See also his *Essais sur la France* (Paris, 1974).

3. A. Sauvy, *La Vie Economique des Français de 1939 à 1945* (Paris, 1978), pp. 196–200.

4. J. P. Rioux, *La France de la 4ème République*, vol. 1 (Paris, 1981), p. 30. Even among the most threatened and most persecuted group in French society, the Jews, a substantial majority, while suffering a terrible calvary, succeeded in surviving. Out of a total of 300 000 Jews living in France in 1939, of whom one half were French Jews and one half foreign Jews, 76 000 – of whom one-third were French Jews and two-thirds foreign Jews – were deported to Germany where they were almost all massacred (only 2500 of them returned). In total, despite the persecution, five-sixths of the French Jewish community and two-thirds of the foreign Jews escaped death. A very different balance sheet from that of the neighbouring occupied countries (in the Netherlands, for example, three-quarters of the Jewish community perished) and *a fortiori* from the almost complete extermination of Jewish communities in Central and Eastern Europe.

5. Alan Milward, *The New Order and the French Economy* (Oxford, 1970), pp. 271–3.

6. To give an idea of the food shortage, one can cite a significant anecdote. Just after the Liberation, a banquet was organised at Montpellier, the menu for which was ennumerated by the *Commissaire de la République* in an official report: 'shredded carrots with one slice of salami, inedible ragoût, approximate cheese'. Cited by J. P. Rioux, *La France*, p. 46.

7. J. Fourastié, 'La population active française pendant la Seconde guerre mondiale', *Revue d'Histoire de la 2ème Guerre Mondiale*, 57, (January, 1965) pp. 14–17.

8. Institut d'Histoire du Temps Présent: Table Ronde 'Les entreprises françaises de 1939 à 1945', November 1986. To be published by the Institute in 1988, edited by R. Frank, P. Fridenson, A. Beltran and E. Dejonghe.

9. H. Frenay, *La nuit finira* (Paris, 1973) p. 117.

10. See the special number of *Vingtième Siècle: revue d'histoire*, 5 (January–March, 1985), in particular the article by Henry Rousso, 'Vichy le grand fossé', pp. 57–79.

11. See M. Baudot, 'L'épuration, bilan chiffré', *Bulletin de l'Institut d'Histoire du Temps Présent*, 25 (September 1986) pp. 37–53. See also C. Lévy, 'L'épuration en France: approche bibliographique', ibid., 4 (June, 1981).

12.   P. Novick, *The Resistance Versus Vichy* (New York, 1968); (French translation, Paris, 1985).
13.   Charles de Gaulle, *Mémoires de Guerre*, vol. III (Paris, 1959) p. 38.
14.   Figures given by P. Guiral in *Les épuration administratives* (Geneva, 1977) p. 103.
15.   François Bédarida, 'Les faux tabous de l'épuration', *Le Nouvel Observateur*, 7–13 November 1986.
16.   F. Bloch-Lainé and J. Bouvier, *La France*, p. 13.
17.   Raymond Aron, *Les conséquences sociales de la guerre*, Cours au Collège Libre des Sciences Sociales et Economiqués, ch. I.
18.   See J. P. Rioux, 'A Changing of the Guard? Old and New Élites at the Liberation', in J. Howarth and P. Cerny (eds) *Élites in France: origins, reproduction and power* (London, 1981).
19.   H. Rousso, 'Les élites economiques dans les années 1940', in *Le élites in Francia e in Italia negli anni quaranta*, (Milan and Rome, 1983), pp. 29–49.
20.   J. Fourastié, 'La Population . . .' p. 8.
21.   F. L. Closon, *Le temps des passions* (Paris, 1976) p. 162.
22.   See C. Andrieu, *Le Programme du Conseil National de la Résistance* (Paris, 1983).
23.   R. Kuisel, *Capitalism and the State in Modern France* (New York, 1981).
24.   A good example in a special area of social work is given in M. Chauvière, *Enfance inadaptée: l'héritage de Vichy*, (Paris, 1987).
25.   See C. Bourdet, *L'aventure incertaine*, (Paris, 1975); F. Bloch-Lainé, *Profession: fonctionnaire* (Paris, 1976); B. Chenot, *Réflexions sur la cité 1945–1980* (Paris, 1981). Already in 1945 a communist journalist had prepared a virulent accusation: P. Hervé, *La Libération trahi*, (Paris, 1945).

7 Women, War and Social Change: Women in Britain in World War II
Penny Summerfield

Twentieth-century wars have been seen not just as periods of social change for women, but as periods of progress towards their emancipation. Contemporaries spoke in these terms. For instance Edith Summerskill wrote in March 1942: 'The freedom which women are enjoying today will spell the doom of home life as enjoyed by the male who is lord and master immediately he enters his own front door.'[1] The view that World War II contributed significantly to the growth of equality between the sexes was popular with historians until relatively recently. In 1974, for example, Arthur Marwick concluded a discussion of the effects of the war on British, American, Russian and German women, by stating that their participation as workers in the war effort 'can be seen at work everywhere in further developments in the status of women'.[2] More recently, historians have become increasingly dismissive of an uncritical reading of this view, and indeed Marwick himself has qualified his earlier position. Gail Braybon argues that the positive effects of World War I on women have been greatly exaggerated, and I put forward a similar argument in a study of the effects of mobilisation and 'dilution' on women in World War I in Britain. Women were recruited and introduced into 'male' industries like engineering, and substitutes were found for women's role in domestic work, cautiously, in the teeth of considerable opposition, as temporary measures to meet an emergency.[3] Leila Rupp's study of mobilisation propaganda in the USA suggests that changes of 'image' there were also superficial, and D'Ann Campbell's detailed study of the effects of mobilisation on American women, counters any easy assumptions that women's job opportunities improved substantially, that pay equalised, or that attitudes to the conventional domestic division of labour changed much. Most recently, Harold Smith has dismissed the idea that World War II saw a rise in the status of British women, attacking suggestions which he attributes to Arthur Marwick that war-time employment was a new experience for most women, that women welcomed the opportunity of doing paid work and entered the labour force voluntarily, that the war undermined the sex segregation of jobs and that war-time employment made women permanently dissatisfied with traditional sex roles.[4]

The attention drawn to the absence of a transformation in women's lives as a result of mobilisation for war has been salutary. Nevertheless the strength of what one might call the 'revisionist' view of women in World War II now tends to obscure the fact that the war did necessitate changes in women's lives, and that it was regarded by many participants as a key phase in terms of personal change and development. Tess, a Labour Supply Officer working for the Ministry of Labour during the war, summed up the feelings expressed by many women invited to reflect on the significance of the war in their lives:

> It seemed to me a tremendous opportunity for women to find out what they could do. Not only in doing the work, but managing their families and affairs while the men were away. I watched a whole lot of women bloom then they found out that they could do all these things that they had been told they couldn't do, and they enjoyed the feeling that they could learn and put their hands to anything that turned up. I watched the older women find that they were necessary. We were all necessary and needed, the country couldn't get on without us. For myself, my own confidence was boosted by tackling things that I'd never done before.[5]

Oral evidence suggests that many women felt that their lives were being profoundly changed even if they did not experience or expect 'emancipation', and that the place of women after the war was not exactly what it had been in 1939, even though many of the war-time changes had been negated.[6] It may be helpful to clarify what the concept of emancipation implies. Feminists are agreed that the root of women's lack of freedom can be traced to the division of society according to sex, and the proscription of women's activities on their side of the division by the expectation that their lives will be dominated by biological functions and caring roles, which are ascribed a low status. They see women's role in the home as primarily one of servicing a male breadwinner as his dependent, bearing and rearing children and caring for other members of the family with little independence in terms of either time or money. In the workplace sexual divisions have meant that single women are viewed as temporary workers, awaiting marriage and the assumption of the conventional wifely role and therefore not worth training and by nature unskilled. Married women have been viewed as secondary members of the workforce, working to supplement incomes primarily earned by their husbands, and therefore appropriate candidates for the lowest paying, least skilled work, with the lowest potential for promotion.

It has been well established (by myself, Smith and others) that World War II did not overturn the identification of women with the roles outlined above, and in this sense did not have an 'emancipating' effect.[7] But this does not rule out the possibility that important changes did take place. What follows is an attempt to explore the ways war-time changes did affect women, which women experienced the greatest changes, and how these war-time disturbances fitted into longer-term trends.

The aspect of the war which appeared strikingly to reduce the difference between men's and women's social roles was the demand for women's labour in the munitions industries and essential services. Before the war, women who worked outside the home were employed mainly in textiles, clothing, routine factory work and especially domestic service, where over 2 million worked in 1931 out of a workforce of about 6 million women. As far as white collar and professional work were concerned numbers of women were tiny in all occupations except nursing, schoolteaching, retailing, and clerical work such as that in the lower grades of the civil service. Between the wars women entered industries like the light metal trades, electrical engineering and scientific apparatus making, in small numbers but at a slightly faster rate than men, so that proportions of women in these industries rose. Women were employed as unskilled or semi-skilled labour in women's sections of these industries, at considerable savings to employers compared with the cost of employing men.[8]

During the war, women were needed particularly urgently in engineering, metals, chemicals, vehicle building, transport, the energy industries and shipbuilding. There was an increase of over 1.5 million women in these 'essential' industries and by 1943 women represented 33 per cent of the total number of employees in them, compared with 14 per cent in 1939. There was also an urgent demand for women as white-collar workers in national and local government, where the number of women expanded by 500 000, raising the proportion from 17 to 46 per cent of the workforce. By September 1943 there were also 470 000 women in the armed forces, and 80 000 in the Women's Land Army. Numbers in the traditional 'women's' industries declined, to the anxiety of the government as far as textiles and clothing were concerned (by the end of 1943 it was desperately trying to reverse the exodus) and to the chagrin of the middle and upper classes in relation to domestic service (as Frances Partridge's diary, *A Pacifist's War*, records). By 1943 at the height of the mobilisation of women, an estimated 7 750 000 women were in paid employment, and at least one million more were enrolled in the Women's Voluntary Service.[9]

To a large extent these war-time changes were reversed afterwards, though some left more of a residue than others. Between 1943 and 1947 there was a decrease of 1 750 000 women in employment, bringing the proportion of all adult women occupied down from 51 per cent in 1943 to 40 per cent in 1947. The downward trend continued to 35 per cent in 1951, close to the 1931 proportion of 34 per cent. Women's employment in the armed forces was all but wiped out, dropping from nearly half a million to just over 60 000 by 1947. But even though there was a fall from the war-time peaks of women in industries which had previously employed them in small numbers, like engineering, vehicles, metals, gas, water and electricity and transport, more women were employed in these industries than had been in 1939. For example, women represented 21 per cent of engineering workers in 1950 compared with 34 per cent in 1943 and only 10 per cent in 1939. They comprised 12 per cent of the metal manufacturing workforce, compared with 22 per cent in 1943 and 6 per cent in 1939, and 13 per cent of transport workers compared with 20 per cent in 1943 and 5 per cent in 1939. Women white-collar workers also held on to some of their gains in national and local government, where the proportion was 38 per cent in 1948 compared with 46 per cent in 1943 and 17 per cent in 1939. The other side of the coin was the decline of personal, 'living-in' domestic service, which never recovered from its war-time depletion. Paid domestic work was by no means dead, however. There was a growing demand for daily chars and office cleaners, whose officially recorded numbers expanded from 158 000 to 238 000 between 1931 and 1951.[10]

The war's contribution to the pattern of women's employment was mainly one of accelerating on-going trends. This applied to the type of work women did, as well as to the industries and occupations in which they worked. The jobs women undertook were rarely recognised as skilled, even when the women were directly replacing men, mainly because of employers' denial of the notion that women were capable of skilled work, their insistence that women needed extra supervision and mechanical assistance, and their assertion that the work women were doing during the war was 'commonly performed' by women in the industry. This last claim enabled them to avoid the clauses of the

'Relaxation Agreements' made with the unions to suspend union opposition to the entry of women during the war, which stated that women replacing men should be paid equal rates to the men and should be regarded as temporary. In defence of their male members' jobs trade unionists fought a rearguard action against the classification of war work as 'women's work' which involved them in disputes over employers' claims that a wide variety of work from sweeping up the factory floor to truck driving and inspection was 'commonly performed' by women in the industry.[11] Women workers themselves objected to the contradiction between the experience of replacing men on all kinds of war work, some of it demanding and dangerous, and that of receiving half or less of the men's earnings. A woman in the fitting shop at Consett Steel Company during the war expressed her outrage 40 years later:

> I was off work for a week – I was ill for a week – and I went back to the shop – fitting shop – and the fella that was on my job for that week got twelve pounds and I was only getting the three and I *said* why should he – I mean, sort of *then* there were the heckles up, you know; I was doing the same job as him exactly. I had the same responsibility; in fact, I had more because it *was* my job and why couldn't I have that? They just pooh-poohed and laughed, you know, and threw you out.[12]

Some women in the technical branches of the Armed Services, who received two-thirds of men's pay, developed a similar sense of grievance, though to have expressed it would have earned them the charge of mutiny.[13] But there were cases of women in industry taking strike action (illegally in war-time) over equal pay with the men they were replacing. The most celebrated strike took place at the Hillington Rolls Royce plant near Glasgow in October 1943. The women did not get equal pay, but instead found that most of them were placed on the lowest rungs of a new sex-related grading scheme.[14] This was the shape of things to come. In 1946 the Royal Commission on Equal Pay refused to recommend equal pay for women manual workers on the grounds that they were, all things considered, less efficient than men. Rather then continuing a system of classifying work simply as 'men's' or 'women's', the unions after the war worked towards grading schemes and job evaluation. It was of course assumed that women's place within these schemes would be in the lowest grades.[15]

During the war the gap between men's and women's earnings

narrowed, but only by a few percentage points. In 1938 women earned 47 per cent, in 1945 52 per cent and in 1955 an estimated 53 per cent of men's average weekly earnings. It was women in white-collar work whose pay position improved most, though inequality was still great. Women clerks received 46 per cent of male clerk's pay in 1935 and 57 per cent in 1955.[16]

Taken together the evidence indicates that there was no transformation of women's employment due to the war. But it would be wrong to believe that the war made no difference, particularly in quantitative terms. One economist calculated that if there had been a return by 1948 to the *status quo* in 1939 'the number of insured women would have fallen by more than 400 000. But in fact the number increased by about 350 000'.[17]

Who were the women in paid work during and after the war? The 'revisionists' are right to draw attention to the fact that most women industrial workers were not 'green' labour unused to paid work.[18] They had transferred from other industries and occupations or re-entered the labour force having left on marriage or the birth of the first child to become full-time housewives. Ninety per cent of the latter group of married women had done paid work at an earlier stage in their lives, though only one-fifth of them had had any intention of returning to paid work.[19] The employment prospects of such women were more profoundly affected by the war than those of any other group.

In 1931 only 16 per cent of working women were married, whereas in 1943 43 per cent were wives, one-third of whom had children under 14. Even though there appears to have been a small fall in the proportion of married women workers immediately post-war, this change outlived the war. In 1947 40 per cent, and in 1951 43 per cent of women workers were married and the proportion had risen to 52 per cent by 1959.[20] As far as age was concerned, before the war the age profile of women workers had been heavily weighted towards the youngest age groups, 41 per cent being under 25, by 1943 only 27 per cent were in this age group, and higher proportions of women over 35 were represented. This redistribution continued post-war. In 1947 only 24 per cent of women workers were under 25 and the age groups over 35 were represented even more heavily than they had been during the war, 49 per cent now being in the age group 35–59 compared with 42 per cent in 1943.[21] Geoffrey Thomas commented that during the war married and older women flocked into paid employment transforming the conventional profile. After the war younger married women moved out, as his and other surveys had predicted, but older married women continued to come into paid work, so the profile did not return to its pre-war shape.[22]

In addition to the expansion in the number of women workers who were married, the proportion of all wives who went out to work rose between the Censuses of 1931 and 1951, from 10 to 22 per cent.[23] Harold Smith seeks to minimise the effect of the war on this increase, by quoting statistics which, he argues, show a steady upward trend from 1931, to which the war contributed a mere 4 per cent.[24] However, his figures for 1939 and 1947, crucial to the argument, are suspect. He derives the proportion of 14 per cent in 1939 from an article by Hilary Land, which purports to draw on Thomas's *Women at Work* (1944), but in fact confuses the proportion of all married women who were employed with the proportion of all employed women who were married.[25] It is only the latter figure which Thomas quotes in *Women at Work*, and he does not give a proportion for 1939. Smith's figure of 18 per cent of all wives who went out to work in 1947 is taken from a table in Political and Economic Planning's report, *Employment of Women* (1948). PEP based its statistics on the Government Actuary's forecast of January 1946 and advised caution in the use of its estimates of the proportions of married, single and widowed women in the female labour force, stating in particular that 'the number of married women in this table may be too small (the possible margin of error is at least 200 000)'.[26] The addition of this figure to its total brings the proportion of married women in employment up to 21 per cent, close to the estimate of 22 per cent in 1947 offered by Thomas in *Women and Industry* (1948),[27] which is equal to the proportion recorded by the Census in 1951. Without reliable figures for 1939 and 1947, as well as for the war itself, it is impossible to be conclusive about the war's effect on the proportion of wives in paid employment. However the suggestion that there was a substantially increased proportion of working wives during the course of the war is consistent with the undisputed war-time rise in the proportion of women workers who were married, and the shift to an older age profile of women workers.

It is reasonable to conclude that the war played a major part in the transition from the pre-war situation in which the majority of women workers were single and nearly half were under 25, to that of the 1950s, when the typical woman worker was the older married women with children.[28] Women were right to feel that their employment opportunities had altered. During the war many households had their first experience of older married women, including mothers of children under 14, going out to work, and this turned out not to be a temporary phenomenon. How did these changes in married and older women's work opportunities come about, and what was their impact on women's position at work and at home?

The caution of policy-makers about mobilising older, married women, and of such women themselves about taking on work outside the home during the war, suggest that the war-time removal of the social divide which had previously prevented large numbers of married and older women from participating in paid work was by no means a foregone conclusion. The government was hesitant about subjecting any women to compulsory mobilisation, even though the call up for men was introduced immediately the war began, under the National Service (Armed Forces) Act of 3 September 1939. Registration of women at labour exchanges and their subsequent direction into work, and the call-up of women under the National Service (Number 2) Act, were not initiated until March and December 1941 respectively, by which time the labour shortage was severe.

Call-up was selective for men, those deemed medically unfit or members of a 'reserved occupation' being exempt. But in addition to these considerations, women's availability was determined by their role within the home. No married woman was subject to call-up under the National Service (Number 2) Act (though it was decided in Cabinet that a single woman who married after she had been conscripted should not be released: 'Any other course', it was said in Cabinet, 'would put a premium on reckless marriages'[29]). And a complex web of exemptions surrounded the direction of wives into work either locally or at a distance under the Registration and Direction scheme, such that even a woman running a 'small household' of only one other adult than herself with domestic help could be exempt. A childless serviceman's wife could not be sent away into war work since it was considered vital that she was available for him in 'his' home, when he returned on leave. Men between the ages of 18 and 41, extended in 1941 to 50, were liable for military serviice, but though Registration applied to all women aged 18–40, only single women aged 20–30 could be 'called up' and sent into the Forces, and unlike men they were, at least theoretically, given the chance to opt instead for industry, the Land Army or Civil Defence. Above all, while fatherhood exempted a man from nothing, no mother of a child under 14 living with her could be directed into war work.[30]

The exemptions suggest that the government's intentions were to obtain as many women workers as possible without upsetting the conventional patterns of domestic work and childrearing, in other words without disturbing the traditional division of labour in the home. There were, after all, over 10 million men in the civilian workforce throughout the war and also some 10 million children under 14.[31] If women did not look after them in the conventional way, who would do so? The answer has to be that the cost to the government of their care, if not performed by women as wives and mothers, would have been enormous. Thus young single women (the conventional female labour force) were the prime target of mobilisation policy. The problem for the government was that this supply was not sufficient to meet war-time needs. Hence the changes introduced in 1943. The age of conscription was lowered from 20 to 19 and the age groups covered by registration were enlarged from an upper limit of 40 to 50, amid shocked press reaction that this amounted to the conscription of grandmothers. In addition the government began to direct previously exempted housewives into part-time work, and to provide those in rural areas with industrial outwork, done in small *ad hoc* workshops or in the woman's own home. Both part-time and outwork were officially organised for the first time in World War II, having existed previously as super-exploitative working arrangements. From 1941 women of all ages, whatever their marital status and degree of domestic responsibility, were urged to volunteer. W. K. Hancock and M. M. Gowing, official historians of the war economy, suggest that mobilisation of the civilian population went further in Britain than in any other combatant country, and they are emphatic about married women's contribution: 'It was largely the enlistment of married women into employment during 1942 and 1943 that made the peak of British mobilisation so very high.'[32]

What can one say about the effects of this mobilisation on women's conventional role in the home? Young single women were more inclined than older married women to welcome it for the new opportunities they hoped it would bring. In particular young middle-class women sought a life in the uniform of the Women's Royal Naval Service, the Women's Auxiliary Air Force, or the Women's Land Army. The Auxiliary Territorial Service, attached to the Army, was not looked upon so favourably, having an image tarnished by allegations of immortality. Work in the ATS was seen as less glamorous too, though in fact there was much routine cooking and clerical work in all three services, as well as some more exciting and responsible jobs, such as searchlight or kinetheodolite operator in the ATS, transport driver or fleet mail censor in the WRNS, and plotter or radio location operator in the WAAFs. Mobility in a relatively high-status, if temporary, job was considered preferable to (and more patriotic than) the continuation through the war of a restricted role as 'daughter of the house'.[33]

There were advocates among women of the idea that married

women should also set aside their conventional roles, at least on a temporary basis. Thus the ease with which wives, especially middle-class wives, could be exempted from war work was increasingly criticised. A strikingly explicit statement on the temporary abandonment of the wifely role was reported to have been made by Lady Reading, the head of the Women's Voluntary Services, in 1944. She beseeched every WVS member to 'forget your home, leave beds unmade, leave the house dirty, don't look after your husband's meals', while throwing herself into war work.[34]

In contrast to those who advocated such change, many married women, including one who wrote to the *Daily Mirror* complaining about Lady Reading's appeal, found that the demands of home and families exerted a stronger pull than those of the state and industry. A Wartime Social Survey undertaken in October 1941 revealed that 32 per cent of a sample of 1000 women apparently available for work would not take up war work, mainly because of their domestic responsibilities and because they disliked the prospect of leaving home. These reasons applied particularly to older married women.[35] Data collected by Mass Observation (MO) suggests that their responses were more complex than simple conservatism. Many were critical of the failure of the government to be explicit about hours, wage rates, and facilities for such things as child care and shopping during the recruitment drive of 1941. They were looking for signs of a willingness to compromise on the part of the government and employers such that they would be able to cope with both a work role and a domestic one. Many were emphatic that their husbands would not tolerate their participation in war work without such a compromise in spite of the extra earnings.[36] Such a view is supported by evidence of men's hostile attitudes towards the mobilisation of 'wives and sweethearts' quoted in Cabinet, Parliament, the press and by Mass Observation. One Coventry wife and mother summed up the situation in describing to Mass Observation how she had requested part-time work at the 'Unemployment Bureau' as she called it in November 1941, but was rebuffed: 'They could give us full-time work but we would get war in our homes if we took it,' she said.[37]

Part-time work, introduced at official insistence from 1943, has a place of considerable significance as an indicator of the government's commitment to mobilising women without upsetting conventional home life and of married women's preference to be mobilised on such terms. At first, as the figures suggest, employers were unenthusiastic about part-time work. Early in 1942 under 20 000 women were engaged under such arrangements and employers responded with horror to the idea that hours should be organised, as they saw it, for the personal convenience of the workers. 'A factory isn't a place where you can drop in for a spot of work just when you feel like it', remarked one Birmingham labour manager to some women applicants, acidly.[38] But once direction of women into part-time work had been introduced in 1943 the number of part-timers rose, reaching 900 000 in 1944.[39] Some of the advantages which employers now saw in it were not so favourable for the women doing it, for instance the most boring and unpleasant work was, on the advice of the Ministry of Labour, given to part-timers, since they were more likely to tolerate it for their shorter hours than full-timers. And part-timers received the lowest wage rates and rarely qualified for bonuses and benefits.[40]

Nevertheless, part-time work was popular with many of those who did it. Fifty-eight per cent of the women asked by the Wartime Social Survey in 1943 said either that they definitely wanted to go on with it or that they might do so, after the war. Women quoted by MO in *The Journey Home* published in 1944 stressed the new freedom they found in part-time work. For example one wife and mother of 40 said: 'I thoroughly enjoy my four hours working here in the afternoon. I'm all agog to get here. After all, for a housewife who's been a cabbage for fifteen years – you feel you've got out of the cage and you're free.' Another part-timer said, 'I wish part-time had come to stay.'[41] In fact it had. In 1947 around one-quarter of women in paid employment were said to be in part-time work and by 1973 the proportion had risen to 34 per cent. The number of part-time women workers was 1.8 million in 1951 and 3.5 million in 1977. As early as 1965 more married women worked part-time than full time.[42]

But although part-time war work brought a welcome change to the lives of such women, it is important to note that it did not fundamentally change the division of labour between husbands and wives. Part-time arrangements made it possible to keep homes going in much the normal way and was widely applauded for precisely this.[43] As part-timers told MO, housework and shopping could be fitted in around working hours, husbands and children could still be given their main meals at home, and the care of young children was easier to arrange for a few hours than for a full day.[44] In other words the inadequacy of the government's provision of 'substitutes' for the housewife did not impose the burden on part-timers which it did on full-timers.

From 1941 government ministries had addressed themselves to the problems for women workers of coping with tasks like child care, shopping, cooking and washing, and had taken some steps on all of them. For example, by September 1944 there were 71 806 nursery places for the under-fives provided jointly by the Ministry of Health and Local Authorities; discussions on shopping schemes had been held by the Ministry of Food with retailers, industrial employers and unions; the government had urged local authorities to provide British Restaurants and required employers to provide canteens in undertakings over a certain size, and laundrywork was rated an essential civilian service from which, by the end of 1942, workers could not be withdrawn.[45] But none of these varieties of substitution for women's domestic work provided a comprehensive service. Policy-makers were reluctant to collectivise normally private domestic functions, and left much to private initiative, usually in the name of the collective war effort. Child care was the area in which intervention was greatest but in December 1941, at a time when the labour shortage was acute, official policy was that women should find their own private childminders, and that nurseries should merely fill the gaps. In spite of the Ministry of Labour's pressure, Medical Officers of Health, responsible for the implementation of nursery policy in localities where there was a demand for married women's labour, frequently denied that there was such a demand or that married women wanted nurseries, sometimes in the face of local campaigns for 'Nurseries for Kids. War Work for Mothers!' They reiterated, 'A mother's place is in the home where she should look after her own children.' At the height of the war effort, in 1943, war-time nurseries accommodated at most one-quarter of the children under five of women war workers.[46]

In the absence of more adequate substitutes the attempt to keep a home and family going and engage in war work was too much for some women. Absenteeism was rife among full-time women workers. At 12 to 15 per cent of working hours it was twice that of men, from 1943 to 1945, and married women lost up to three times as much time as single women, which government investigators attributed mainly to domestic responsibilities. In contrast there was little absenteeism among part-time workers. Women's turnover rates were between 0.8 and 0.92 per cent per week in the munitions industries in 1943 meaning that a firm would have to recruit nearly half its female labour force a year to maintain the current level of employment.[47] Wartime publicists were being misleading when they suggested that, in spite of bombing, rationing, shortages and all the other aspects of war which made housekeeping specially difficult, married women in full-time war work heroically bore the double burden without complaint. They took time off consistently to make it possible to do the two jobs and left work when the burden became to great.

Did the strain of the war-time double burden mean that the 'new' women workers of World War II were anxious to leave work as soon as peace arrived? Publications on the post-war world projected an image of women longing to leave factory work for wife and motherhood, and official demobilisation policy was based on the assumption that this would be the case. Ministry of Labour officials were instructed to direct young women to take the place of older ones who were presumed to be waiting anxiously to be released from industry. In particular, women with young children were not expected to go on working. Nurseries were being closed throughout 1945, wherever the Ministry of Health could sustain the claim that they were underused, and the Treasury subsidy was halved from the beginning of 1946. Few local authorities were committed to continued support of day nurseries, especially since they were bound by the 1944 Act to provide nursery schools (open during school hours for three to five year olds only) where there was local demand. The proportion of children in any sort of pre-school institution returned to its pre-war level, and if mothers wanted or needed to go out to work, they had, even more than during the war, to resort to minders.[48]

In fact the majority of women surveyed did want to stay in paid work after the war. Sixty-six per cent of women in an Amalgamated Engineering Union survey of 1944–5, three-quarters of whom had entered the industry during the war, said they wanted to stay in engineering, and this included 79 per cent of married women who had not been in paid employment immediately before the war, and 86 per cent of those over 40 years of age.[49] The most thorough of the surveys of women's attitudes to post-war work were those undertaken by Geoffrey Thomas of the Government Social Survey in 1943 and 1947, to which references have already been made. His 1943 survey reported that a minimum of 55 per cent and a maximum of 80 per cent of women workers wanted to stay in paid work post-war (the latter figure included those who gave conditional answers such as 'if possible' and 'might have to'). In spite of the difficulties of shouldering the double burden during the war this included a large number of wives. The proportion of married women who wished to work either full- or part-time was 39 per cent, compared with 36 per cent of married women who definitely did not want to go on working post-war. The rest were uncertain, most of them saying that it depended how much their husbands were earning or on their economic circumstances generally. Married women with children showed an even stronger intention to work, 49 per cent of them wishing to carry on working either full-time (36 per cent) of part-time (13 per cent). Thomas found in 1947 as well as 1943 that being a mother of children over five was not a disincentive to doing paid work. On the contrary children provided a compelling economic reason for going out to work.[50]

Who were the women who emphatically did not want to go on working post-war? In 1943 only 7 per cent of all single women came into this category and they were concentrated in the younger age groups (up to 34). Two-thirds of them were intending to get married. The other major group which definitely wanted to leave war work consisted of married women in the same age groups. Forty-three per cent of those aged 18–24 and 25–34 intended to give up paid work, mostly because they had 'enough to do at home'. Thomas's findings in 1947 confirmed the pattern predicted in 1944. The advent of marriage and devotion to a home and husband in its early years were the most important reasons for giving up paid work. They were more important than children. However, married women over the age of 35 evidently found the idea of full-time housewifery both less attractive and less binding than younger ones.[51]

What had war-time mobilisation given these women that they wanted to hang on to? In 1943 women surveyed named 'the money' and 'the company' as the aspects of doing war work they valued most and the same was true of those surveyed in 1947.[52] Women would obviously lack both of these if they engaged only in unpaid domestic work in their homes. Even though, contrary to the myth of war-time equal pay, women did not earn as much as men, a woman's own earnings gave her a measure of independence which many women, especially wives, had not had pre-war. As one woman put it to Mass Observation, 'When you get up in the morning you feel you go out with something in your bag, and something coming in at the end of the week, and it's nice. It's a taste of independence and you feel a lot happier for it.'[53] Together, income and work-mates constituted major sources of the confidence which many women have referred to as the main legacy of the war in personal terms. How long that feeling lasted after the war must have varied enormously. There was considerable job loss among women from 1944 as war production shifted its emphasis, and much readjustment at the end of the war. For example, clerical workers such as bank clerks had the experience of having to train returning men to take their war-time places on the counter, after which the women were expected to return to the backrooms once more. In some industries like steel-making and shipbuilding (where product demand was high post-war and there was not a labour surplus) women stayed on into the late 1940s and even in the 1950s, but when redundancies arrived, as they did in engineering during 1945, shop stewards made sure women would be the first to be dismissed. Furthermore some women were under pressure from their returning husbands not to go out to work any more. The figures showing the expansion of employment for older married women during and after the war should not be read as indicating unbroken continuity for individuals. As Geoffrey Thomas put it, 'The changes are the result of a continuous inflow and outflow of women over the years.'[54]

The surveys reported broad public agreement on the idea that men should be breadwinners, that marriage could be an alternative to earning her own living for a woman, and that married women 'should go out to work only if they could carry out their duties to their homes and families'.[55] Harold Smith is right, therefore, to point to the absence of a transformation of the sexual division of labour within marriage during the war. But the surveys reviewed above do not support the view that the majority of married women 'fervently wish themselves back into their pre-war way of life', a suggestion made in 1943 by Margaret Goldsmith which Smith endorses.[56] It is all too easy to emphasise, as contemporaries did, the feelings of women who were tired of war work and looked forward to full-time domesticity. But it is important to differentiate between the attitudes of younger and older married women towards paid work after the war and to give due weight to those who were considering carrying on with paid work post-war, who in fact outnumbered those who definitely did not want to do so.

Was the war's 'most important legacy for women' really 'a strengthening of traditional sex roles rather than the emergence of new roles' as Smith concludes?[57] Even some women who did not intend to continue in paid work after the war but looked forward to the resumption of their roles as full-time homeworkers felt that the experience of war work meant that they would not return to being quite the same sort of housewives as they had been before. For example, Zelma Katin wanted to give up her part-time work on the Sheffield buses when her husband came out of the Army, but was determined to have a 'more interesting life' than she used to lead and believed that this would depend on husbands and wives co-operating within the home more than ever before. And Nella Last knew that her voluntary work for the WVS would come to an end but resolved never again to let her husband's needs and moods dominate her. The war was vital to her in giving her the opportunity to insist on greater independence, including a room of her own.[58] Both Zelma and Nella would have endorsed Summerskill's statement with which this chapter opened.

To settle the issue of the extent to which the war contributed to changes in marital styles one would need considerably more evidence than is at present available.[59] Mass Observation did produce a report on 'The State of Matrimony' in 1947 based on surveys of attitudes to marriage undertaken in 1945 and 1947. The report reflects the war-time restlessness of women about conventional marital styles but does not attempt to quantify it, and also suggests that changes were slow to emerge from dissatisfaction. For example, the authors stated,

> Throughout our work on marriage and family life the recurrent grumble we have found has concerned the wife being tied to the house, loss of freedom of movement and an inability to take part in the outside pleasures and amusements of single life. A diminishing number of husbands agree with the one of sixty-five years who, when asked what he and his wife had in common replied, 'A wife's place is indoors'. But wives still stay indoors.[60]

Some groups concerned about the falling birthrate urged changes within marriage such that women would no longer feel so trapped (e.g. greater sharing between spouses, and also the contribution that could be made by local authority babysitters, home helps, day nurseries and better housing).[61] But official ideology was not behind the new-style marriage. The advice given to the 'returning soldier' did not present equality in marriage as an ideal. One publication warned the demobilised soldier that his wife was likely to have a 'pleasant feeling of independence and self-confidence' as a result of having managed during his absence, but that he should 'resume his rightful place as breadwinner of the household' as soon as he could.[62] As Denise Riley shows in *War in the Nursery*, the campaign to give wives greater freedom was contradicted in the same body of 'pronatalist' literature by the proscription of a wife's destiny to that of a full-time mother bearing major responsibility for the physical and psychological development of her children in a conventional marriage within which she and the children were provided for by her husband. In a similar way, Beveridge's emphasis on marriage as an equal partnership in his proposals for post-war social insurance was contradicted by the actual position of married women in his plan. A wife was dependent on her husband's contributions and on the benefits he received on her behalf.[63]

Harold Smith dismisses the apparent changes in marital styles as no more than an aspiration which flared up among a few women during the war, to be quenched by the return of their menfolk afterwards.[64] Certainly post-war evidence such as it is, suggests that the doom

Summerskill predicted befalling the dominant paterfamilias was not universal. The incidence of the development of 'companionate' marriages varied according to social class, region and occupational group, with highly segregated marriages persisting particularly in areas of heavy industry. But Jane Lewis argues that companionship, sharing and mutual sexual satisfaction were increasingly stressed by couples before and after World War II, although she warns that 'the equality of tasks and responsibilities that began to be envisioned for husbands and wives after World War II was in practice often associated with subordinate and superior status.'[65] The basic structure of marriage had not changed, but even if women found that maintaining a sharing relationship between a breadwinner husband and domestic wife was hard in the post-war years, it was a marital objective which was markedly different from those of most women's mothers and grandmothers. It would seem perverse to suggest that the stress under which war placed marriage made no contribution to this long-term shift.

War-time rates of illegitimacy and divorce should throw light on the effect of the war on marriage. Illegitimacy rose from 4.4 per cent of all live births in 1939 to 9.1 per cent in 1945, the main change being that fewer extra-marital conceptions were legitmated by marriage than before,[66] and there was a four-fold increase in the number of divorce petitions filed for adultery between 1939 and 1945. Before the war over half the petitions had been submitted by wives but during and after it husbands filed more than wives. For both partners there was an increase in opportunities for infidelity during the war, perhaps particularly for wives, especially in the presence of 4.5 million British and 1.5 million overseas servicemen stationed all over the country in the run-up to D-day. Divorces numbered 15 221 in 1945 and reached the huge total of 58 444 in 1947.[67] The possibility of obtaining divorce more cheaply and expeditiously than ever before through the Army Welfare Service, in the context of pre-war legislation liberalising the divorce laws,[68] made a major contribution to the rising number of decrees nisi granted. But as with the illegitimacy statistics, so with divorce, the figures are indicative of a population forced to be highly mobile, in which there had been considerable disturbance of conventional patterns of courtship and marriage. At least some divorces were the result of the stresses caused by efforts to alter relationships within marriage. Many wives bore testimony in the problem pages of women's magazines, as they have since in oral history interviews, to the difficulties of reconciliation with husbands after the period of separation or involvement in separate areas of war-related activity. Mrs Cheshire of Lancaster terminated her pre-war marriage at the end of the war. Her comment was: 'Mind you if the war hadn't come along and we hadn't been separated I suppose it would have been gelled out of custom.'[69]

The other side of the picture was the recovery of the marriage rate at the end of the war[70] and the high birth rate, reaching 20.7 births per thousand of the population in 1947, compared with only 14.4 in 1941,[71] both of which suggest that the war had not diminished the attractiveness of marriage and family to either sex. But the situation was perhaps not quite as 'retrogressive' for women as Smith argues.[72] The trend towards small families consisting of two children close in age, born during the early years of increasingly youthful marriages, was not reversed by the baby bulge. It was a crucial condition of the availability of women in their thirties and forties for paid work, and was vital to the post-war establishment of the M-shaped curve of women's labour force participation, peaking at ages 18 and 44.[73]

The acute labour shortage which prevailed during the war played a vital role in expanding the supply of older, married women who were prepared to put up with the double burden in order to go out to work, preferably on a part-time basis. But did it make the married woman worker a more acceptable social phenomenon? Married women received conflicting messages. They were urged by the Ministry of Labour to take manual work during its campaign of 1947, and in 1948 and after married women with teaching qualifications (previously excluded by the marriage bar) were urged to rejoin the profession, to help meet the growing demand for teachers caused by the introduction of universal secondary education, the raising of the school leaving age to 15 and population growth.[74] To some publicists it was a matter of social duty for married women with children of school age or older to undertake paid work, at least on a part-time basis.[75] On the other hand the ideology that a married woman's first duty was to her home and children was still paramount. Indeed the war had barely dented it and post-war pronatalist arguments about the primacy of motherhood in a woman's life reinforced it, bolstered by theories of the psychological damage to children of married women 'leaving' home to go out to work, and by the images of domestic femininity which pervaded the consumerism of the 1950s.[76]

Did the war alter employers' attitudes to married women workers? The question is one on which historians offer different interpretations. Using a Civil Service Report of 1946 on the marriage bar, Cmd 6886, which included a small survey of the practices of other employers, public and private, and the governments of seven other countries,

Arthur Marwick argues that the war had caused employers to change their opinion in favour of married women as employees, whereas Harold Smith argues that most employers still believed that married women had 'definite disadvantages' as workers.[77] The picture presented in the report is in fact not clear-cut. Though all the British public and private employers had taken on married women during the war there was indecision among them about whether they would continue to do so afterwards. Four out of fifteen said they would, four that they would not, four had not decided, and three said that they might make exceptions in individual cases. Sheffield City Council, one of the four who regarded married women as having disadvantages and which was undecided about the future, said tellingly that its post-war practice would 'depend on the state of the labour market'.[78] The Civil Service made a similar pragmatic response. The authors of the report complained that during the war married women 'have tended to be absent or unpunctual becasue of domestic responsibilities or the difficulty of getting domestic help; they have needed time off for shopping; and they have taken leave at very short notice when their husbands came home on leave from the forces';[79] but in 1946 the bar was dropped throughout the Civil Service, with the exception of Foreign Service.[80]

In as far as one can draw a general picture it seems to be that married women had been recruited hesitantly in the course of the war, and that they were retained reluctantly at its end by all employers apart from a few who regarded them as steadier and more productive than 'flighty' single women.[81] Increasingly, demographic changes meant that employers had no choice. The rising rate of marriage and the falling age at which women married, coupled with dwindling cohorts of the younger age groups due to the low birth rate in the inter-war years, meant that it would be possible to fill labour force requirements only by using older married women.[82] Their 'handicaps' did have the advantage of vindicating employers' remuneration practices. The consensus among employers who presented evidence to the Royal Commission on Equal Pay in 1945 was that the high rates of absenteeism and turnover characteristic of married women justified the relatively low rates paid to women in general. Even the three women 'dissenters' among the Commissioners did not rush to the defence of the married woman worker. Their arguments were oriented towards the exceptional 'committed' single woman. Why should she be penalised by the inefficiency and unreliability of those who should not really be at work at all, since they belonged in the 'natural and traditional sphere of women's work, housekeeping and the care of children'? Their views were in keeping with those of the Women's Advisory Committee to the Trades Union Congress. Married women, above all mothers of young children, should not need to work.[83]

In conclusion, I have emphasised the war's contribution to the expansion of opportunities for older and married women to engage in paid work, particularly through the establishement of part-time working arrangements as a normal employment practice. This was a major change for many women. Casual work had of course existed before the war, and women continued to take jobs like charring, childminding and numerous types of homework, still largely uncounted. But part-time work in factories, offices, schools and hospitals offered the older married women who took it up less housebound lives than their pre-war equivalents, even though there is little evidence to suggest that it assisted the breakdown of sexual divisions at work or at home. Whether one is talking about manual or white-collar work, married women's part-time work since the war has had the lowest status and has been the lowest paid. The war may have accelerated the rise of the companionate marriage, and the readiness to dissolve an unsatisfactory one, but although such a change in style was important in terms of the way the marital relationship was experienced, it did not remove the fundamental division of economic and social roles between men and women. In short, woman's participation in the war effort did not doom the conventional sexual division of labour, though it did assist her involvement in the world of paid work on terms that did not threaten her responsibility for the domestic sphere. It also constituted an experience of major personal importance for many women, which has been largely hidden and forgotten since the war. It would not do for revisionist historians to contribute to this obliteration.

Notes

1. Edith Summerskill, 'Conscription and Women', *The Fortnightly* (March, 1942).
2. A. Marwick, *War and Social Change in the Twentieth Century* (London, 1974) p. 137.
3. G. Braybon, *Women Workers in the First World War* (London, 1981); Penny Summerfield, *Women Workers in the Second World War, production and patriarchy in conflict* (London, 1984).
4. L. J. Rupp, *Mobilizing Women for War, German and American*

Propaganda 1939–1945 (Princeton, 1978); D'Ann Campbell, *Women at War with America, Private Lives in a Patriotic Era* (Cambridge, Mass, 1984); H. L. Smith, 'The effect of the war on the status of women' in H. L. Smith (ed) *War and Social Change, British Society in the Second World War* (Manchester, 1986) p. 211.

5.   P. Schweitzer, L. Hilton and J. Moss (eds) *What Did You Do in the War, Mum?* (London, 1985) p. 30. Comparable accounts were given by women interviewed for the Thames TV/Channel 4 series 'A People's War' (e.g. transcripts of Barbara Davies, Hetty Fowler, Mona Marshall, Clara Moore, Therese Roberts, Joan Shakesheff, Mickey Hutton Storie, Mrs Wheeler). See also oral evidence quoted in Kath Price and Eric Wade, *What did you do in the War, Mam? Women steel workers at Consett during the Second World War* Open University, Northern Region, Working Paper No. 2, June 1984.

6.   For an account of women in both wars largely based on personal testimony, see G. Braybon and P. Summerfield, *Out of the Cage, Women's Experiences in Two World Wars* (London, 1987).

7.   See Summerfield, *Women Workers*; Smith, 'The effect of the War'; Denise Riley, *War in the Nursery, Theories of the Child and Mother* (London, 1983); Margaret Allen, 'The Domestic Ideal and the Mobilization of Womanpower in World War II', *Women's Studies International Forum*, vol. 6., no. 4 (1983).

8.   Census of England and Wales, 1921, *Occupation Tables* (London, 1924), Census of England and Wales, 1931, *Occupation Tables* (London, 1934); C. E. V. Leser, 'Men and Women in Industry', *Economic Journal* (1952) p. 330.

9.   G. M. Beck, *Survey of British Employment and Unemployment 1927–1945*, (Oxford University Institute of Statistics, 1951), Tables 40 and 41; Central Statistical Office, *Statistical Digest of the War* (London, 1951), pp. 9 and 16; H. M. D. Parker, *Manpower* (London, 1957), pp. 323,459, 496; F. Partridge, *A Pacifist's War* (London, 1983); J. M. Hooks, *British Policies and Methods of Employing Women in Wartime* (Washington, 1944) p. 24.

10.   Geoffrey Thomas, *Women and Industry, An Inquiry into the problem of recruiting women to Industry carried out for the Ministry of Labour and National Service*, Central Office of Information, Social Survey, March 1984, p. 6; Guy Routh, *Occupation and Pay in Great Britain 1906–1960* (Cambridge, 1965), Table 20; Summerfield, *Women Workers*, Table B.7, p. 199; Routh, *Occupation and Pay in Great Britain 1906–1979* (London, 1980) p. 39.

11.   See Summerfield, *Women Workers*, ch. 7.

12.   Price, *What Did You Do . . . ?*, p. 30. Emphasis and spelling as in original.

13.   Author's interview with Aline Whalley, WRNS flight mechanic, Royal Naval Fleet Air Arm, 1943–1945, March 1986.

14.   Parliamentary Papers (P. P.), *Report by a Court of Inquiry concerning a Dispute at an Engineering Undertaking in Scotland, 1943*, Cmd. 6474; P. Inman, *Labour in the Minitions Industries* (London, 1957) pp. 364–6.

15.   P. P., Royal Commission on Equal Pay, *Report*, 1946, Cmd. 6937, p. 111, para. 345 passim; Inman, *Labour*, pp. 366–7.

16. Parker, *Manpower*, p. 503; Routh, *Occupation* (1980) p. 123.
17. Leser, 'Men and Women', p. 335.
18. Summerfield, *Women Workers*, p. 30; Smith, 'The effect of the war', p. 212.
19. Geoffrey Thomas, *Women at Work. The attitudes of working women toward post-war employment and some related problems. An inquiry made for the Office of the Minister of Reconstruction*, Central Office of Information, Wartime Social Survey, June 1944, p. 10.
20. Census, 1931, *Occupational Tables*, Table 1; Thomas, *Women at Work*, pp. 1 and 4; Thomas, *Women and Industry*, pp. 6–7 (confusingly Thomas states 'There is no difference between the overall proportions of married, single and widowed women employed in 1943 and 1947' in spite of quoting 40 per cent married in 1947 compared with 43 per cent in 1943); Routh, *Occupation* (1965) p. 47. See also M. Klein, *Britain's Married Women Workers* (London, 1965) graph 11, p. 28.
21. Census, 1931, *Occupational Tables*, Table 3; Thomas, *Women at Work*, p. 1; Thomas, *Women and Industry*, p. 6.
22. Thomas, *Women and Industry*, pp. 6–7.
23. A. H. Halsey, *Trends in British Society since 1900* (London, 1972) Table 4.7.
24. Smith, 'The effect of the war', pp. 218–9.
25. H. Land, 'Women, Supporters or Supported?' in D. Leonard Barker and S. Allen, *Sexual Divisions and Society* (London, 1976) p. 116.
26. Political and Economic Planning, *Planning*, vol. xv, no. 285 (July 1948) 'Employment of Women', p. 58. See also table on p. 39.
27. Thomas, *Women and Industry*, app. 1, p. 30.
28. J. Lewis, *Women in England 1870–1950. Sexual Divisions and Social Change* (Brighton, 1984) p. 218.
29. PRO Lab 65/20, 121st Conclusions, 28 November 1941.
30. On mobilisation policy, see Summerfield, *Women Workers*, ch. 3, and also M. Allen, 'The Domestic Ideal', pp. 405–407.
31. Central Statistical Office, *Statistical Digest*, Tables 9 and 3.
32. W. K Hancock and M. M. Gowing, *British War Economy* (London, 1949) p. 459. See also Summerfield, *Women Workers*, pp. 142–6 on recruitment of part-timers and outworkers.
33. Central Office of Information, Wartime Social Survey, *An Investigation of the attitudes of women, the general public and ATS personnel to the Auxiliary Territorial Service*, October 1941; author's interview with A. Whalley; interview of Marjorie Wardle, driver and later Fleet Mail Officer, WRNS 1942–1946, by M. Easterby-Smith, March 1986; Thames TV interview transcripts (Mickie Hutton Storie, searchlight operator ATS, Therese Roberts, ATS member of Anti-Aircraft battery); Age Exchange, *What did you do . . .?* pp. 14, 17, 19.
34. A. C. H. Smith, *Paper Voices, The Popular Press and Social Change, 1935–1965* (London, 1975) pp. 113–4. See also Summerfield, *Women Workers*, p. 51, n. 88.
35. Wartime Social Survey, *An Investigation*, pp. iii, 6.
36. Mass Observation Archive, (M-OA), File Reports 615, March 1941; 625, April 1941; 952, November 1941; 1238, May 1942, and TC 32, 'Women in Wartime', Box 1, e.g. comments recorded 21 October 1941, 25 November 1941.

37. M-OA, TC 66/4/C-H, War Work Coventry, 1941. See also PRO Cab 65/20, 110th Cabinet Conclusions, 28 November 1941; *Hansard* v 382, c 1296 and v 382, c 1300.

38. Mass Observation, *People in Production: an enquiry into British war production* (London, 1942) p. 177. See also *Engineer*, 30 October 1942.

39. Parker, *Manpower*, p. 182; Hancock and Gowing, *British War Economy*, p. 454.

40. PRO Lab 8/634, . . . Part-time women . . . in the engineering industry, October 1942–January 1943.

41. Mass Observation, *The Journey Home* (London, 1944), p. 58; Thomas, *Women at Work*, pp. 4 and 5.

42. Thomas, *Women and Industry*, pp. 3 and 12; Routh, *Occupation* (1980) p. 46; Lewis, *Women*, p. 219; Klein, *Britain's Married Women Workers*, Table 3, p. 30.

43. e.g. PEP, *Employment of Women*, p. 38: 'Arrangements for part-time work can do much to enable motherhood to be combined with employment without hurt either to the mother or to her child.'

44. MO, *Journey Home*, p. 58.

45. S. Ferguson and H. Fitzgerald, *Studies in the Social Services*, (London, 1954) p. 190, n. 1; Summerfield, *Women Workers*, ch. 5; Hancock and Gowing, *British War Economy*, pp. 444,459.

46. PRO Lab 26/58, . . . Wartime nurseries . . . 1940–2, Stirling to Whyte, 9 October 1941; Summerfield, *Women Workers*, ch. 4, esp. pp. 78 and 84.

47. PRO Lab 26/131, . . . Enquiry into absence from work 1942–3, 13 February 1945; Hooks, *British Methods*, p. 10; Inman, *Labour*, p. 209.

48. See MO, *Journey Home*, pp. 54–6; Parker, *Manpower*, pp. 261–3; Ministry of Labour and National Service, *Report for the War Years*, pp. 167–9; Riley, *War*, pp. 120–2; Summerfield, *Women Workers*, p. 191, and n. 3 and 4.

49. Amalgamated Engineering Union, *Report of the Proceedings of 26th National Committee* June–July 1945, para. 47.

50. Thomas, *Women at Work*, pp. 12a–13; *Women and Industry*, pp. 3, 8 and 12.

51 Thomas, *Women at Work*, pp. 12a, 13; *Women and Industry*, p. 3,7.

52. Thomas, *Women at Work*, p. 20; *Women and Industry*, pp. 18–20.

53. M-OA, File Report 2059, March 1944, p. 4.

54. Schweitzer *et. al.*; *What did you do?*, Price, *What did you do?*, p. 27; pp. 32–2; MOLNS, *Report*, Appendix XVIII (B); Routh, *Occupation* (1980) p. 39; Summerfield, *Women Workers* p. 160; Thames TV transcript, Clara Moore; Thomas, *Women and Industry*, p. 7.

55. Thomas, *Women and Industry*, p. 3. See also M-OA, File Report 2059, p. 8.

56. Smith, 'The effect of the war', p. 225.

57. Ibid.

58. Zelma Katin, *'Clippie': The Autobiography of a War-time Conductress* (London, 1944) pp. 49 and 123; R. Broad and S. Fleming (ed.) *Nella Last's War, a mother's diary 1939–45* (Bristol, 1981) p. 229.

59. Smith complains that Marwick's only example of a woman whose attitudes to men and marriage were changed by the war was Nella, ('The effect of the war' p. 211), but does not in fact offer any *counter* evidence of the same quality.

60. M-OA, File Report 2495, June 1947, p. 17.
61. Riley, *War*, pp. 167–8.
62. K. Howard, *Sex Problems of the Returning Soldier* (Manchester, n. d. [1945]), pp. 62–3.
63. P. P., *Report by Sir William Beveridge on Social Insurance and Allied Services*, Cmd 6404, 1942–3, VI, p. 53. See also J. Lewis, 'Dealing with Dependency: State Practices and Social Realities 1870–1945' in J. Lewis (ed.) *Women's Welfare/Women's Rights* (London, 1983).
64. Smith, 'The effects of the war', p. 211.
65. Lewis, *Women*, p. 79. For a useful survey of post-war literature on marital styles see A. Marwick, *British Society since 1945* (Harmondsworth, 1982), pp. 67–71.
66. Central Statistical Office, *Statistical Digest*, Table 4; Ferguson and Fitzgerald, *Studies*, pp. 90–4.
67. P. P., Royal Commission on Marriage and Divorce, *Report*, Cmd 9678, 1951–55; Thames TV transcript, Hetty Fowler.
68. In 1937 desertion, cruelty and insanity became grounds for divorce.
69. Transcript of Mrs M. Cheshire, Oral History of Girlhood Project, University of Lancaster, 1986. See also Thames TV transcripts, Kitty Murphy, Hetty Fowler, Miriam Power; Schweitzer, *What did you do . . . ?*, p. 52.
70. The figures for the number of marriages per thousand of the population in England and Wales are as follows: 1938: 17.6; 1940: 22.5; 1943; 14; 1945; 18.7. (Ferguson and Fitzgerald, *Studies*, p. 18, n. 1).
71. Central Statistical Office, *Statistical Digest*, Table 4; Ferguson and Fitzgerald, *Studies*, p. 19.
72. Smith, 'The effect of the war', pp. 221–2.
73. Klein, *Married Women*, graph 111, p. 41.
74. Ministry of Education, *Report of the Working Party on the Supply of Women Teachers*, (1949) p. 5.
75. See Riley, *War*, p. 176.
76. Ibid; Birmingham Feminist History Group, 'Feminism as Femininity in the 1950s?' *Feminist Review*, 11, Autumn 1979; C. L. White, *Women's Magazines 1693–1968* (London, 1970), esp. ch. 6.
77. A. Marwick, 'My Battle with the Second World War', *Times Higher Education Supplement*, 6 March 1987, p. 11; Smith, 'The effect of the war', p. 220.
78. P. P., 'Marriage Bar in the Civil Service', *Report of the Civil Service National Whitley Council Committee*, Cmd 6886, 1945–6, app.
79. Ibid, ch. IV, para. 23.
80. N. A. Franz, *English Women Enter the Professions* (Cincinnati, 1965) p. 151.
81. MO, *War Factory*, (London, 1943), p. 26; MO, *People in Production*, pp. 166–7; P. P., Cmd 6886, app. (Boots Pure Drug Company).
82. Klein, *Britain's Married Women*, p. 27; A. Myrdal and V. Klein, *Women's Two Roles, Home and Work* (London, 1968) p. 12.
83. P. P., Royal Commission on Equal Pay, *Report*, see esp. p. 111 and Memorandum of Dissent; Trades Union Congress, Pamphlets and Leaflets, 1942/7, app. 1, and 1943/16, app. 1.

Conclusion
Arthur Marwick

What then have we learned with respect to the nine areas of social change I identified in the Introduction? Here I shall simply do a quick run through the list. But let us first, briefly, see how far the notion of 'societies at war' being affected by forces of change different from, or more intense than, those in play in 'societies not at war' worked out in practice. In doing so we shall of course run up against the principle, known to all historians, that no 'system' will ever fully account for historical processes in all the nuanced complexity with which they actually operate; in the end we have to confront the unique circumstances of each society affected in its own particular way by the war being waged (a complexity which has been so carefully delineated by each specialist contributor).

Not surprisingly (since it is the most palpable aspect of war) every chapter, explicitly, or implicitly, features the destruction and disruption of war, with destruction almost beyond comprehension being described by Paul Dukes in his chapter on the Soviet Union. For the French nation, says James McMillan, World War I 'was a material and moral calamity' with the result that 'post-war France was a very different place' from France of *la belle époque*. On the whole McMillan does not see much of the disaster syndrome (rebuilding better than before) coming into play, though he does note the paradox that 'human disaster' for the peasants in some ways improved conditions for the survivors. In general he is sceptical on the issue of the circumstances of war projecting women into new situations, the 900 per cent expansion of women's employment in the metal industries, for instance, being essentially a temporary phenomenon: he does however draw our attention to the potential long-term significance of unchaperoned bourgeois girls visiting the war-wounded (perhaps one could generalise that while job changes can readily be reversed changes in attitude and moral behaviour are less easily cancelled). The fullest exposition of the possibilities of change inherent in the disruptiveness of war occurs in Mark Roseman's chapter on World War II Germany. War was 'the continuation of tourism by other means' (Paul Dukes makes the same point even more graphically when

119

he writes of Russian soldiers: 'It was difficult to keep them down on the collective farm now that they had taken Berlin'); war, Roseman adds, 'drained' German society, preparing it for the acceptance of a new American-style capitalist society.

The idea of war as test recurs throughout the book, though at times (and this is a most important general point) the test element is seen as provoking complacency rather than change. McMillan writes that 'the régime and the social order it represented had been vindicated' (how passionately one could say the same thing of Britain and World War II[1]); Dukes declares: 'Soviet Society as a whole had passed the test of total war, and its apologists could now proclaim again with enthusiasm their belief in the fundamental rightness of the teachings of Marx, Lenin and Stalin.' While François Bédarida stresses that the test of World War II affected French attitudes more deeply than French institutions, he does bring out very clearly the discarding of 'failed' Third Republic and Vichy political and business leaders, and, above all, the decision, after years of hesitancy, to go for a strong *dirigiste* State. However, it is in the Germany of World War I, as described by Wolfgang Mommsen, that the test effect is at its most forceful, 'dramatically' changing the economy.

The notion of participation is, as pointed out in the Introduction, most fully developed by Alastair Reid who sees it as the primary explanation of the real gains the British working class made in World War I. Again James McMillan is sceptical, though he does record the improvements in girls' education and the new willingness of working-class women to stand up for themselves in taking strike action. But perhaps the most interesting exposition is that of Penny Summerfield who, in discussing women's employment in World War II Britain, shows that you have, as it were, to scrutinise the statistics within the statistics (another important general lesson). While she emphasises that the proportion of adult women in employment, standing at 34 per cent in 1931, having risen to 51 per cent in 1943, was back at 35 per cent in 1951, she goes on to show (previous commentators have usually retired contented at this point) that there were critical long-term gains in such employments as engineering, transport and white-collar work, and, still more critically, that there was a transformation in the employment pattern for married women. With James McMillan, discussing women in another country in an earlier war, she very properly insists that the image and the reality of women's 'proper' roles did not change, but she does, using oral testimony in particular, give an appropriate weighting to the quite crucial changes women themselves felt had taken place in their own lives. Do historians, I sometimes ask myself, really know better than the people they are studying? Readers will have noted for themselves the way in which the participation aspect of war, often merely a barely-stated shadow, flits across the other pages of this book.

That war is indeed a profound psychological experience, exciting, tragic, 'traumatic' (a much favoured word), is abundantly demonstrated in almost every chapter. World War I, McMillan tells us, left 'deep psychological scars' on the French people. For their counterparts in World War II, however, to quote one of Bédarida's central contentions: 'changes in mentalities and collective culture under the shock of war generated in the aftermath a dynamic transformation, which can be expressed in terms of structure, quantitative development and institutional processes. In other words World War II affected the soul still more than the body of France, liberating new energies for new ventures.' On my reading of my colleagues' analyses, at any rate, the psychological dimension of war emerges as one of the most imporant stimulants of such lasting social change as they are prepared to attribute to total war.

Let us now turn to our reckoning of this change. In the area of *social geography* most nations in both wars did undergo considerable relocation of industry, not, however, a matter developed in the chapters of this book, though Mommsen does stress the way in which the exigencies of war intensified the decline of German agriculture. More central, though more difficult to deal with, is the question of demographic change. Most certainty attaches to the effects of World War I on the British population: citing the authoritative researches of Jay Winter, Reid brings out that, as a result of general increases in domestic levels of consumption, death rates were either static or fell by several percentage points. The hazards of the whole subject are brought out be the highly contrasting French experiences of the two wars. Before World War I the French population was already in relative decline so that the wholesale destruction of potential fathers alluded to by McMillan had serious consequences in intensifying France's demographic problems. Yet World War II was accompanied and succeeded, as Bédarida indicates, by a rise in the birthrate. Here we tread among the deepest mysteries with which historians have to cope. World War II was much less directly destructive of human life, but much more disruptive; psychologically it was an entirely different experience: whether or not some of the explanation is to be found here, the facts themselves are of crucial importance. So too is the fact

of immense population movement in Germany at the close of World
War II: Roseman brings out the importance of refugee labour in the
German economic recovery.

The most thorough treatments of *economic change* engendered by
war are to be found in the chapters by Mommsen and Bédarida,
though, we must register, both strongly emphasise the continuities,
Bédarida citing the recent researches of Fridenson and others which
show that economic activity in the 1930s was not as depressed as has
traditionally been believed. Since the outcomes of the two wars are so
manifestly different it is evident that other factors than the various
consequences of waging total war were at work – not least conscious
political action. But it is hard to escape the conclusions that World War
I was the crucial prelude to the depression of the 1920s and 1930s,
while World War II was an important, though not sufficient,
pre-condition of post–1945 economic growth. The question of war's
relationship with the fostering of technological advance is not one
investigated in this book. Complacency was indeed fostered in
post–1945 Russia, but that competition with America and the rest of
the world high-lighted by Dukes has clearly resulted in the same period
in quite impressive technological advance. The two sides of the debate
in regard to British reactions to World War II are clearly set out in
books by Sidney Pollard (who sees Britain emerging from the war with
her technological potential greatly enhanced) and Corelli Barnett
(who sees Britain's woeful inadequacies devastatingly exposed).[2] I
find Pollard the more persuasive; but then I would, wouldn't I?

The study of the relationship of war to changes in *social structure* has
been bedevilled by the recourse frequently made to one of those fatuous
metaphors so beloved by social scientists, 'levelling' (another general
lesson: in studying this subject cast 'levelling' and 'emancipation' into
the dustbin of historiography). A brief reflection on what the word
'levelling' really means will bring out that if classes really were
'levelled' they would cease to exist. All that happens in war is (at least
potentially) an alteration in the relationships between classes.
Mommsen goes into this in some detail in his critique of Kocka's
over-simplified formulations: briefly, big capitalists gained,
landowners lost; the working class, particularly in its organisational
aspects, made some gains, despite widespread privation; both the old
professional middle class and the small tradesmen did very badly. Reid
apprises us of considerable gains for the British working classes as a
consequence of World War I, while, in a very complex, but entirely
persuasive account, Roseman shows how the status of German

workers went up as a result of the many-faceted experiences of World War II, while, at the same time, they developed a willingness to cooperate with capitalist employers. The same war brought to France, in the words of Bédarida, 'a new social balance'.

As the question of ethnic minorities does not quite have the significance in the countries studied here that it had in Austria-Hungary and has in the United States, I'll set the issue of *social cohesion* on the side, though I shall need, when I come to the final topic, *political values*, to recall Mommsen's remarks about lower-middle-class alienation from the Weimar Republic. With regard to *social welfare* McMillan recognises in post World War I France improvements in working hours and in education, while Reid refers to 'important legislative and political changes' in Britain. Again the story in World War II Germany which, as Roseman neatly puts it, had already endured years of 'total peace', is difficult and ironic: but there can be no doubt that the final outcome in post-war capitalist Germany was a form of Welfare State. On France Bédarida is direct and positive: 'there was a social and economic *new deal*, formed by the triangle, Social Security – Nationalisation – Planning. The aspiration towards a new social order both reformist and progressive, in place of the '*désordre établi*' of the pre-war years and the paternalism of Vichy, thus issued in a Welfare State *à la Française*: an enduring state of affairs and one to which the French today are very much attached . . .'

In assessing changes in *material conditions* we have, in essence, to strike a balance between the destructive effects of war and the various 'progressive' processes discussed in my Introduction. Apart from, or indeed in spite of, mass unemployment (Reid and Winter agree), the British people were better off in the 1920s and 1930s than they had been in Edwardian times. For the other countries the destructiveness of war probably outweighed any possible gains. World War II, as we know, ushered in an era of material prosperity. The realm of *customs and behaviour* is one of the most intriguing ones: we have already picked up interesting hints with regard to the lifestyles and behaviour of women from McMillan and Summerfield; Bédarida suggests a great liberating of the spirit in France at the close of World War II and also (here there is overlap with my next topic) a new influence for a new type of Catholicism. Had this been a bigger book there would have been much more to say; interested readers could always turn to my own writings.[3] There too they will need to turn for *intellectual and cultural* change, which was outside the scope of this book, save for the important emphasis Bédarida gives to religious change and Dukes's interesting clue to one of the ways in which war may affect literary sensibility, in his quotation from the novelist Vasily Grossman who wrote of 'the distortion of the sense of time during combat.'

Changes in the *role and status of women*, on the other hand, have been very fully discussed. McMillan, Bédarida and Summerfield all bring out very clearly that neither war changed the traditional framework of marriage and notions of women's proper place in society. Summerfield points out that while the new pattern of older married women working part-time in the years after the World War II represented a very real and welcome change for the women themselves, its effect was to consolidate the traditional marriage (though perhaps slightly altering relationships within that marriage); she also comes down very clearly against the position taken by Harold L. Smith that the war did not increase employment possibilities for married women.[4] Dukes shows that the representation of women in the Soviet Communist party increased sharply during World War II. And, from out of the transformations of that same war, French women did at last get the vote. One can see clearly why, in the end, they did not get the vote in 1919 or 1920; but one must ask the 'revisionists' why they did get it in 1945 and not in 1935 or 1955.

Finally, *social and political values, institutions and ideas*. The changes of régime at the end of World War I are too obvious to have been elaborated on in this book; both Roseman and Bédarida, however, go into careful detail in discussing the new régimes which came into being in, respectively, Germany and France at the end of World War II. But perhaps the most fascinating argument is that of Mommsen: 'during the First World War a cluster of socio-economic factors and mental orientations emerged which provided a seedbed for extreme nationalism and, eventually, for the rise of National Socialism to power.'

But the purpose of a collection of this sort is not to impose check-lists or patterns, but to bring out the diversity of experience as between the different countries, and to demonstrate the complex and, at times, almost impenetrable inter-relationship between war and the many other forces bearing upon a country's social development. Alastair Reid wisely suggested that the mechanisms touched off by the exigencies of war are more likely to result in 'progressive' social change in liberal countries than in autocratic ones; the extent to which destruction negates any other more positive forces also seems to be critical. The particular problem of a Germany already under a semi-military, but also 'revolutionary', régime is brought out by

Roseman: 'In general we can say that the war undermined the Nazi's own appeal while reinforcing many of the social changes which they had initiated in the thirties.' Roseman also provides a sharp summing-up: 'It is evident that "total war" is not an independent cause of social change. Its influence on German society was shaped decisively by the nature of the régime which waged it and that of the régime which followed it.'

On the whole then, the long-term trends, as they should, have it. But there is a warning in Roseman's words: neither Nazism nor the advent of an American-style régime can be described as 'long-term trends'; they are, rather, immediate political and ideological contingencies. And then we must remember that Mommsen attributes very much of the rise of Nazism to World War I; while only the collapse in war of Nazi Germany permitted the creation of the new régime. So wars do play a crucial part in the manner and timing of important developments and events; it would be impossible to understand the history of Europe in the twentieth century without understanding the complex legacies of two total wars.

Notes

1. Marwick, *War and Social Change*, p. 165; 'Problems and Consequences of Organizing Society for Total War', p. 21; 'Total War and Social Change in Britain and other European Countries'.
2. Sydney Pollard, *The Wasting of the British Economy* (London, 1982), p. 124; Corelli Barnett, *The Audit of War: The Illusion and Reality of Britain as a Great Nation* (London, 1986), esp. chs 8 and 9.
3. e.g. *War and Social Change*, pp. 92–6.
4. Harold L. Smith, 'The effect of the war on the status of women' in *War and Social Change: British Society in the Second World War*, (Manchester, 1986), pp. 218–22.

Annotated General Bibliography

(This Bibliography is confined to books relating to the general issues raised in the Introduction and Conclusion, together with a few books dealing with those cultural and intellectual matters which have not been very fully explored in this book: for specialist bibliographies see the notes to the individual chapters.)

ADDISON, Paul, *The Road to 1945: British Politics and the Second World War* (1975) scholarly study which perceives a shift in politics and attitudes to social reform caused by the experience of war.

ANDRESKI, Stanislaw, *Military Organisation and Society* (1954) this was the work which gave birth to the notion of a *Military Participation Ratio*; as mentioned in the Introduction, the simpler notion of Participation seems to me more fruitful.

AZEMA, Jean-Pierre, *From Munich to the Liberation, 1938–1944* (1984) good text book of France and World War II.

BECKET, Ian F. W. and SIMPSON, Keith, (eds) *A Nation in Arms: A Social Study of the British Army in the First World War* (1985) very properly draws attention to the experiences of soldiers themselves, supporting the view (see Introduction) that soldiers, being under an authoritarian regime, benefit less than civilian sectors of society from *participation*: 'conceivably', Becket puts it, 'wars change societies more than the armies that defend them.'

BERGONZI, Bernard, *Heroes Twilight* (1980) discussion of World War I writers.

BERKIN, Carol R. and LOVETT, Clara M., *Women, War and Revolution* (New York, 1980) feminist and 'revisionist'.

BERNARD, Philippe, *La Fin d'un monde 1914–1929* (Paris, 1975) as the title suggests, sees the effects of World War I on France as essentially negative.

BLYTHE, Ronald, (ed.) *Writing in a War* (1982) collection of World War II writings.

BRAYBON, Gail, *Women Workers in the First World War* (1981) feminist and 'revisionist', though recognises the effects of war in raising women's 'consciousness'.

CADWALLADER, Barry, *Crisis of the European Mind* (1981) discusses influence of World War I on intellectuals.

CRUICKSHANK, John, *Variations on Catastrophe* (1982) concerned with the intellectual and cultural impact of World War I.

DLUGOBORSKI, Woclaw (ed.) *Zweiter Weltkrieg, Sozialer Wandel* (Göttingen, 1981) a wide range of specialist papers relating to Germany and German-occupied Europe.

FELDMAN, Gerald D., *Army, Industry and Labor* (New York, 1966) a key work in bringing out the significance of *participation* for the position of German labour.

FERRO, Marc, *The Great War* (1973) includes subtle analysis of war's effects on mentalities; sees Russian Revolution as the major consequence of the war.

FLORINSKY, Michael, *The End of the Russian Empire* (1931) an older, and perhaps slightly simplistic, work which stresses the way in which the Tzarist regime failed to meet the *test* of World War I.

FUSSELL, Paul, *The Great War and Modern Memory* (1975) a classic study of the effect of World War I on English literature.

GREENWALD, Maureen Weiner, *Women, War and Work: The Impact of World War I on Women Workers in the United States* (Westport, Connecticut, 1980) straightforward balanced study of American women's participation of World War I.

HARDACH, Gerd, *The First World War* (1977) stresses continuities and sees the Russian Revolution as the single most significant consequence of World War I.

HARRIES, Meiron and Susie, *The War Artists: British Official War Art of the 20th Century* (Joseph, in Association with the Imperial War Museum and the Tate Gallery, London, 1983) a useful survey.

HARRIS, Frederick, J., *Encounters with Darkness* (1983) discussion of European literature in World War II.

HARTMANN, Susan, *The Home Front and Beyond: American Women in the 1940s* (Boston, 1982) feminist and 'revisionist'.

HAVENS, Thomas R., *Valley of Darkness: The Japanese People and World War II* (New York, 1978) the treatment of social change is extremely brief, but nonetheless offers some interesting comparative insights.

HIGONNET, Margeret Randolph, JENSON, Jane, MICHEL, Sonia and WEITZ, Margaret Collins, *Behind the Lines: Gender and the Two World Wars* (1987) long, very feminist collection of very short essays, preceded by an assertively revisionist introduction.

HONEY, Maureen, *Creating Rosie the Rivetter: Class, Gender, and Propaganda during World War II* (Amhurst, 1984) the title is sufficiently illuminating.

HOWARD, Michael, 'Total War in the 20th Century: Participation and Consensus in the Second World War', in *War and Society: A Yearbook of Military History* (edited by Brian Bond and Ian Roy, 1976) elegant brief survey by Britain's leading figure in war studies.

ISENBERG, Michael T., *War on Film* (New York, 1981) concerned with America and World War I.

KATKOV, George, *Russia 1917* (1967) brings out the significance of the *participation* of the 'voluntary organisations' of middle-class citizens in Russia during World War I.

KLEIN, Holger, (ed.) *The First World War in Fiction* (1976) one of many such useful collections.

KOCKA, Jürgen, *Facing Total War: German Society 1914–1918* Leaming Spa, (1984) written from a Marxist perspective, and concentrating largely on the lower middle class, its thesis that the war pushed that class down into the proletariat, is challenged in Mommsen's chapter.

LASKA, Vera, *Women in the Resistance and the Holocaust: The Voice of Emptiness* (Westport, Connecticut, 1983) important and balanced contribution.

LEED, Eric J., *No Man's Land: Combat and Identity in World War I* (1979) highly original work discussing how soldiers themselves were affected by waging war.

MACNICOL, John, *The Movement for Family Allowances 1918–1945* (1980) the chapter dealing with World War II is strongly 'revisionist'.

MAIER, Charles S., *Recasting Bourgeois Europe: Stabilisation in France, Germany and Italy in the Decade after World War I* (1975) very much a 'revisionist' work.

MICHEL, Henri, *Les Courants de pensée de la résistance* (Paris, 1964) of all Michel's works, this is perhaps the one which brings out most clearly the relationship between the experience of war and ideas of social change.

MICHEL, Henri, *The Second World War* (1975) a thousand pages of comprehensive coverage.

MICHEL, Henri and MIRKINE-GETZOVITCH, Boris, *Les Idées politiques et sociales de la résistance* (1954) an invaluable collection of documents bringing out the relationship between the Resistance and social reform.

MILWARD, Alan, *The German Economy at War* (1965) a standard authority.

MILWARD, Alan, *The Economic Effects of the World Wars on Britain* (1970) takes the line that of all countries Britain was the least affected by total war.

MILWARD, Alan, *The New Order and the French Economy* (1970) standard work of economic rather than social orientation.

MILWARD, Alan, *War, Economy and Society, 1939–1945* (1977) basically an economic survey, this offers a judicious conclusion on the social effects of the Second World War: 'the economic, social and psychological experience of war produces a change in the climate of social consciousness.'

MOMMSEN, Wolfgang J., (ed.) *The Emergence of the Welfare State in Britain and Germany* (1982) contains a number of specialist essays which deal with the effects of war, some taking a 'revisionist' stance some not.

PAUL, Wolfgang, *Der Heimatkrieg* (Esslingen, 1980) a rare study.

POLENBERG, Richard, *War and Society: America 1941–1945* (New York, 1972) clearly indicates areas where World War II brought significant change.

PUGH, Martin, *Electoral Reform in War and Peace, 1906–18* (1978) the classic statement of the case that World War I hindered rather than helped women's suffrage in Britain; thus a 'revisionist' work.

REILLY, Catherine W., *Scars upon my Heart* (1981) discusses women's poetry from World War I.

RUPP, Leila, *Mobilising Women for War: German and American Propaganda, 1939–1945* (Princeton, 1978) a central study in the feminist canon, strongly 'revisionist' in effect.

SCHMITT, Bernadotte E., *The World in the Crucible* (New York, 1984) comprehensive study of Europe and World War I.

SILKIN, John, *The Penguin Book of First World War Poetry* (1979) one of several such useful collections.

SMITH, Harold L., *War and Social Change: British Society in the Second World War* (Manchester, 1986) this is a splendid collection of meticulous and illuminating essays drawing upon up-to-the-minute research which (as it seems to me) is less monolithic in arguing the case that the war brought little significant social change than the editor claims, so scrupulous are the individual authors in presenting the evidence.

STEVENSON, John, *British Society 1914–1945* (1982) balanced, but broadly 'revisionist' in tone.

SUMMERFIELD, Penny, *Women Workers in the Second World War* (1984) one of the most important 'revisionist' works dealing with Britain.

THANE, Pat, (ed.) *The Origins of British Social Policy* (1978) 'revisionist' in attitude towards the effects of war.

THEBAUD, F., *La femme au temps de la guerre de 14* (Paris, 1986) feminist but scarcely 'revisionist'.

TIPPETT, Maria, *Art in the Service of War* (1984) concerned with Canada and World War I.

TRAVERS, Martin, *German Novels of the First World War and their Ideological Implications, 1918–1933* (1982) the scope is well defined by the title.

VANSITTART, Peter, *Voices from the Great War* (1981) one of many such collections, letting us hear something of what participants, rather than historians, had to say.

WAITES, Bernard, *War and a Class Society 1910–1920* (Leamington Spa, 1987) perceives some substantive changes in the position of the working class within the English class structure, due to the effects of World War I.

WILLIAMS, J, *The Home Fronts: Britain, France and Germany 1914–1918* (1972) rather traditional general account.

WILSON, Elizabeth, *Only Halfway to Paradise: Women in Post-war Britain, 1945–1968* (1980) moderately 'revisionist'.

WILSON, Trevor, *The Myriad Faces of War: Britain and the Great War 1914–1918* (Cambridge, 1986) huge and comprehensive study which avoids engaging with the main debate, save for denying, without much discussion of the implications of the term, that World War I for Britain was a *total war*.

WINTER, J. M., *The Great War and the British People* (1986) with impressive statistical underpinning, refutes much of the 'revisionist' case.

WOHL, Robert, *The Generation of 1914* (1980) studies what intellectuals themselves wrote about the changes wrought in their lives through their war experiences.

WRIGHT, Gordon, *The Ordeal of Total War 1939–1945* (New York, 1969) a standard work which grapples seriously with the question of relationship between war and social change.

WYNN, Neil A., *From Progressivism to Prosperity: World War I and American Society* (New York, 1986) a masterly analysis which most effectively pins down the war's effects as 'two steps forward and one step backwards'.

Index

134 *Index*